CASSEROLES

SIMPLE & DELICIOUS HOME COOKING

pil

Publications International, Ltd.

Photograph on page 3 copyright © Shutterstock.com. All recipes and other photographs copyright © Publications International, Ltd.

Pictured on the front cover: Sausage, Potato and Apple Bake *(page 57)*.

Pictured on the back cover *(clockwise from top right):* Vegetable Quinoa Frittata *(page 5)*, Spinach-Cheese Pasta Casserole *(page 174)*, Carmel Chicken Fresco Bake *(page 98)* and Ramen Tamale Pie *(page 31)*.

ISBN: 978-1-64030-062-0

Manufactured in China.

8 7 6 5 4 3 2 1

Microwave Cooking: Microwave ovens vary in wattage. Use the cooking times as guidelines and check for doneness before adding more time.

CONTENTS

BREAKFAST & BRUNCH

VEGETABLE QUINOA FRITTATA

MAKES 6 SERVINGS

1 tablespoon olive oil

1 cup diced onion

1 cup small broccoli florets

¾ cup finely chopped red bell pepper

2 cloves garlic, minced

1¼ teaspoons coarse salt

¼ teaspoon black pepper

1½ cups cooked quinoa

¼ cup sun-dried tomatoes, chopped

8 eggs, lightly beaten

¼ cup grated Parmesan cheese

1 Preheat oven to 400°F.

2 Heat oil in large ovenproof nonstick skillet over medium-high heat. Add onion and broccoli; cook and stir 4 minutes, Add bell pepper; cook and stir 2 minutes. Add garlic, salt and black pepper; cook 30 seconds, stirring constantly. Stir in quinoa and sun-dried tomatoes.

3 Gently stir in eggs; cook until softly scrambled. Sprinkle with cheese.

4 Bake about 7 minutes or until eggs are set. Let stand 5 minutes before serving.

SPICY SAUSAGE POPOVER PIZZA

MAKES 8 SERVINGS

8 ounces turkey breakfast sausage patties, crumbled

8 ounces ground turkey

⅓ cup chopped onion

1 clove garlic, minced

¾ cup chopped red bell pepper

1½ cups all-purpose flour

¼ teaspoon salt

¼ teaspoon red pepper flakes

1 cup milk

3 eggs

1 cup (4 ounces) shredded Cheddar cheese

½ cup (2 ounces) shredded mozzarella cheese

½ cup pizza sauce

1 Preheat oven to 425°F. Spray 13×9-inch baking dish with nonstick cooking spray.

2 Combine sausage, ground turkey, onion and garlic in large skillet; cook and stir over medium heat until turkey is browned. Drain fat. Stir in bell pepper.

3 Combine flour, salt and red pepper flakes in large bowl. Whisk milk and eggs in medium bowl until blended; whisk into flour mixture until smooth. Pour into prepared baking dish; sprinkle with sausage mixture and cheeses.

4 Bake 21 to 23 minutes or until puffed and golden brown.

5 Meanwhile, place pizza sauce in small microwavable bowl; microwave on HIGH 1 minute. Top each serving with 1 tablespoon pizza sauce.

CHEDDAR AND LEEK STRATA

MAKES 12 SERVINGS

8 eggs

2 cups milk

½ cup porter ale or stout

2 cloves garlic, minced

¼ teaspoon salt

¼ teaspoon black pepper

1 loaf (16 ounces) sourdough bread, cut into ½-inch cubes

2 small leeks, coarsely chopped

1 red bell pepper, chopped

1½ cups (6 ounces) shredded Swiss cheese

1½ cups (6 ounces) shredded sharp Cheddar cheese

1 Spray 13×9-inch baking dish with nonstick cooking spray.

2 Whisk eggs, milk, ale, garlic, salt and black pepper in large bowl until well blended.

3 Spread half of bread cubes in prepared baking dish; sprinkle with half of leeks and half of bell pepper. Top with ¾ cup Swiss cheese and ¾ cup Cheddar cheese. Repeat layers. Pour egg mixture evenly over top.

4 Cover tightly with plastic wrap or foil. Weigh down top of strata with slightly smaller baking dish. Refrigerate at least 2 hours or overnight.

5 Preheat oven to 350°F. Bake, uncovered, 40 to 45 minutes or until center is set. Serve immediately.

FETA BRUNCH BAKE

MAKES 4 SERVINGS

1 medium red bell
  pepper

2 packages (10 ounces
  each) fresh spinach,
  stemmed

6 eggs

1½ cups (6 ounces)
  crumbled feta
  cheese

⅓ cup chopped onion

2 tablespoons chopped
  fresh parsley

¼ teaspoon dried dill
  weed

Dash black pepper

1 Preheat broiler. Line broiler pan or baking sheet with foil.

2 Place bell pepper on prepared pan. Broil 4 inches from heat source 15 to 20 minutes or until blackened on all sides, turning every 5 minutes. Place in paper bag; close bag and set aside to cool 15 to 20 minutes. Remove core; cut bell pepper in half and rub off skin. Rinse under cold running water. Cut into ½-inch pieces.

3 Fill medium saucepan half full with water; bring to a boil over high heat. Add spinach; return to a boil. Boil 2 to 3 minutes or until wilted. Drain and immediately transfer to bowl of cold water. Drain spinach; let stand until cool enough to handle. Squeeze to remove excess water; finely chop.

4 Preheat oven to 400°F. Spray 1-quart baking dish with nonstick cooking spray.

5 Beat eggs in large bowl with electric mixer at medium speed until foamy. Stir in roasted pepper, spinach, cheese, onion, parsley, dill weed and black pepper. Pour into prepared baking dish.

6 Bake 20 minutes or until set. Let stand 5 minutes before serving.

EGG AND GREEN CHILE RICE CASSEROLE

MAKES 4 SERVINGS

¾ cup uncooked instant brown rice

½ cup chopped green onions

½ teaspoon ground cumin

1 can (4 ounces) diced mild green chiles, drained

¼ teaspoon salt

4 eggs, beaten

½ cup (2 ounces) shredded sharp Cheddar cheese or Mexican cheese blend

¼ cup pico de gallo

1 medium lime, quartered

1 Preheat oven to 350°F. Spray 8-inch square baking dish with nonstick cooking spray.

2 Cook rice according to package directions; stir in green onions and cumin. Spread in prepared baking dish.

3 Sprinkle chiles and salt over rice mixture. Pour eggs evenly over top.

4 Bake 30 to 35 minutes or until center is set. Sprinkle with cheese; bake 3 minutes or until cheese is melted. Let stand 5 minutes before cutting. Serve with pico de gallo and lime wedges.

MUSHROOM AND ONION EGG BAKE

MAKES ABOUT 6 SERVINGS

1 tablespoon vegetable oil

4 ounces sliced mushrooms

4 green onions, chopped

1 cup cottage cheese

6 eggs

1 cup sour cream

2 tablespoons all-purpose flour

½ teaspoon salt

⅛ teaspoon black pepper

Dash hot pepper sauce

1 Preheat oven to 350°F. Spray shallow 1-quart baking dish with nonstick cooking spray.

2 Heat oil in medium skillet over medium heat. Add mushrooms and green onions; cook and stir until tender.

3 Place cottage cheese in food processor or blender; process until almost smooth. Add eggs, sour cream, flour, salt, black pepper and hot pepper sauce; process until blended. Stir in mushrooms and onions. Pour into prepared baking dish.

4 Bake 40 minutes or until knife inserted near center comes out clean.

BAKED PUMPKIN FRENCH TOAST

MAKES 6 SERVINGS

1 tablespoon butter, softened

1 loaf challah or egg bread (12 to 16 ounces), cut into ¾-inch-thick slices

7 eggs

1¼ cups whole milk

⅔ cup canned pumpkin

1 teaspoon vanilla

½ teaspoon pumpkin pie spice

⅛ teaspoon salt

3 tablespoons sugar

2 teaspoons ground cinnamon

Maple syrup

1 Generously grease 13×9-inch baking dish with butter. Arrange bread slices in dish, fitting slices in tightly.

2 Whisk eggs, milk, pumpkin, vanilla, pumpkin pie spice and salt in medium bowl until well blended. Pour over bread in prepared baking dish; turn slices to coat completely with egg mixture. Cover and refrigerate 8 hours or overnight.

3 Preheat oven to 350°F. Combine sugar and cinnamon in small bowl; mix well. Turn bread slices again; sprinkle generously with cinnamon-sugar.

4 Bake about 30 minutes or until bread is puffy and golden brown. Serve immediately with maple syrup.

ROASTED PEPPER AND SOURDOUGH BRUNCH CASSEROLE

MAKES 8 SERVINGS

3 cups sourdough bread cubes

1 jar (12 ounces) roasted red pepper strips, drained

1 cup (4 ounces) shredded sharp Cheddar cheese

1 cup (4 ounces) shredded Monterey Jack cheese

1 cup cottage cheese

6 eggs

1 cup milk

¼ cup chopped fresh cilantro

¼ teaspoon black pepper

1 Spray 11×7-inch baking dish with nonstick cooking spray.

2 Place bread cubes in prepared baking dish. Arrange roasted peppers evenly over bread cubes; sprinkle with Cheddar and Monterey Jack cheeses.

3 Place cottage cheese in food processor or blender; process until smooth. Add eggs and milk; process just until blended. Pour over ingredients in baking dish; sprinkle with cilantro and black pepper. Cover and refrigerate 4 hours or overnight.

4 Preheat oven to 375°F. Bake, uncovered, 40 minutes or until center is set and top is golden brown.

HAM AND CHEESE BREAD PUDDING

MAKES 8 SERVINGS

1 small loaf (8 ounces) sourdough, country French or Italian bread, sliced

3 tablespoons butter, softened

8 ounces ham or smoked ham, cubed

1 cup (4 ounces) shredded Cheddar cheese

3 eggs

2 cups milk

1 teaspoon ground mustard

½ teaspoon salt

⅛ teaspoon white pepper

1 Spray 11×7-inch baking dish with nonstick cooking spray.

2 Spread one side of each bread slice with butter. Cut into 1-inch cubes; place on bottom of prepared baking dish. Top with ham; sprinkle with cheese.

3 Beat eggs in medium bowl. Whisk in milk, mustard, salt and pepper until blended. Pour egg mixture evenly over bread mixture; cover and refrigerate at least 6 hours or overnight.

4 Preheat oven to 350°F. Bake, uncovered, 45 to 50 minutes or until puffed and golden brown and knife inserted into center comes out clean. Serve immediately.

BLUEBERRY-ORANGE FRENCH TOAST CASSEROLE

MAKES 6 SERVINGS

½ cup milk

⅓ cup sugar

4 eggs

1 tablespoon grated orange peel

½ teaspoon vanilla

6 slices whole wheat bread, cut into 1-inch pieces

1 cup fresh blueberries

1 Preheat oven to 350°F. Spray 8-inch square baking dish with nonstick cooking spray.

2 Whisk milk and sugar in large bowl until sugar is dissolved. Add eggs, orange peel and vanilla; whisk until well blended. Add bread and blueberries; toss to coat. Pour into prepared baking dish; let stand 5 minutes.

3 Bake 40 to 45 minutes or until top is browned and center is almost set. Let stand 5 minutes before serving.

SIESTA RAMEN STRATA

MAKES 12 SERVINGS

- 3 packages (3 ounces each) ramen noodles, any flavor*
- 2 cups (8 ounces) shredded Cheddar cheese
- 10 large eggs, lightly beaten
- 4 cups milk
- ¼ cup finely chopped red bell pepper
- 2 tablespoons chopped green onions
- 1 tablespoon chopped fresh cilantro
- 1 teaspoon salt
- ⅛ teaspoon ground red pepper
- Sour cream, sliced avocado or salsa (optional)

Discard seasoning packets.

1 Spray 13×9-inch baking dish with nonstick cooking spray.

2 Split each noodle square horizontally into two pieces; line baking dish with noodle squares. Sprinkle with cheese.

3 Whisk eggs, milk, bell pepper, green onions, cilantro, salt and ground red pepper in large bowl until well blended. Pour over cheese and noodles. Cover and refrigerate 4 to 6 hours.

4 Preheat oven to 350°F. Bake, uncovered, 50 to 60 minutes or until knife inserted into center comes out clean. Serve with sour cream, avocado or salsa, if desired.

TIP: For a spicier flavor, add ¼ to ½ teaspoon chili powder to the egg mixture.

HASH BROWN CASSEROLE WITH BACON

MAKES 12 SERVINGS

- 1 package (32 ounces) refrigerated diced potatoes
- 1 container (16 ounces) sour cream
- 1 can (10¾ ounces) condensed cream of chicken soup, undiluted
- 1½ cups (6 ounces) shredded sharp Cheddar cheese
- ¾ cup thinly sliced green onions
- 4 slices bacon, crisp-cooked and crumbled
- 2 teaspoons hot pepper sauce
- ¼ teaspoon garlic salt

1 Preheat oven to 350°F. Spray 13×9-inch baking pan with nonstick cooking spray.

2 Combine potatoes, sour cream, soup, cheese, green onions, bacon, hot pepper sauce and garlic salt in large bowl; mix well. Spread evenly in prepared pan.

3 Bake 55 to 60 minutes or until potatoes are tender and cooked through. Stir before serving.

CRUSTLESS HAM AND ASPARAGUS QUICHE

MAKES 6 SERVINGS

- 2 cups sliced asparagus (½-inch pieces)
- 1 red bell pepper, chopped
- 1 tablespoon water
- 1 cup milk
- 2 tablespoons all-purpose flour
- 2 eggs
- 2 egg whites
- 1 cup chopped cooked deli ham
- 2 tablespoons chopped fresh tarragon or basil
- ½ teaspoon salt
- ¼ teaspoon black pepper
- ½ cup (2 ounces) finely shredded Swiss cheese

1 Preheat oven to 350°F.

2 Combine asparagus, bell pepper and water in medium microwavable bowl; cover with waxed paper. Microwave on HIGH 2 minutes or until vegetables are crisp-tender. Drain vegetables.

3 Whisk milk and flour in large bowl. Add eggs and egg whites; whisk until well blended. Stir in vegetables, ham, tarragon, salt and black pepper. Pour into 9-inch pie plate.

4 Bake 35 minutes. Sprinkle cheese over quiche; bake 5 minutes or until center is set and cheese is melted. Let stand 5 minutes before serving.

VARIATIONS: Add 1 clove minced garlic and/or 2 tablespoons chopped green onion to the egg mixture.

BEEF

RAMEN TAMALE PIE

MAKES 6 SERVINGS

- 2 teaspoons vegetable oil
- 1 small onion, chopped
- 1 jalapeño pepper, minced*
- 1 pound ground beef
- 1 can (about 14 ounces) fire-roasted diced tomatoes
- 1 package (3 ounces) beef-flavored ramen noodles, crumbled
- 1 teaspoon ground cumin
- 1 cup frozen corn
- 1 package (8½ ounces) corn muffin mix
- ⅓ cup milk
- 1 egg
- ½ cup (2 ounces) shredded Cheddar cheese

*Jalapeño peppers can sting and irritate the skin, so wear rubber gloves when handling peppers and do not touch your eyes.

1 Preheat oven to 400°F.

2 Heat oil in large skillet over medium heat. Add onion and jalapeño; cook and stir 4 minutes or until softened. Add beef; cook and stir 6 to 8 minutes or until browned, stirring to break up meat. Drain fat.

3 Add tomatoes, seasoning packet from ramen noodles and cumin; mix well. Remove from heat; stir in corn and half of ramen noodles. Transfer to 9-inch square baking dish.

4 Combine muffin mix, milk and egg in large bowl; mix well. Spread over beef mixture; sprinkle with cheese and remaining noodles.

5 Bake 30 to 35 minutes or until corn bread is golden brown and cooked through.

IT'S A KEEPER CASSEROLE

MAKES 4 SERVINGS

1 tablespoon vegetable oil

½ cup chopped onion

¼ cup chopped green bell pepper

1 clove garlic, minced

2 tablespoons all-purpose flour

1 teaspoon sugar

½ teaspoon salt

½ teaspoon dried basil

½ teaspoon black pepper

1 package (about 16 ounces) frozen meatballs, thawed

1 can (about 14 ounces) whole tomatoes, cut up and drained

1½ cups cooked vegetables (any combination)

1 teaspoon beef bouillon granules

1 teaspoon Worcestershire sauce

1 can (12 ounces) refrigerated buttermilk biscuits

1 Preheat oven to 400°F.

2 Heat oil in large saucepan over medium heat. Add onion, bell pepper and garlic; cook and stir 5 minutes or until vegetables are tender.

3 Add flour, sugar, salt, basil and black pepper; mix well. Add meatballs, tomatoes, vegetables, bouillon and Worcestershire sauce; cook and stir until slightly thickened and bubbly. Transfer to 2-quart casserole; arrange biscuits on top.

4 Bake 15 minutes or until biscuits are golden brown.

STROGANOFF CASSEROLE

MAKES 8 SERVINGS

1 package (16 ounces) uncooked egg noodles

2 cans (10¾ ounces each) condensed cream of mushroom soup, undiluted

1 container (8 ounces) sour cream

½ cup milk

1 pound ground beef

2 cans (6 ounces each) sliced mushrooms, undrained

1 package (8 ounces) cream cheese

1 package (about 1 ounce) gravy mix

1 Preheat oven to 350°F.

2 Cook noodles according to package directions in Dutch oven. Drain well; return to Dutch oven.

3 Add soup, sour cream and milk to noodles; mix well. Cover and keep warm.

4 Brown beef in large skillet over medium-high heat 6 to 8 minutes, stirring to break up meat. Drain fat. Add mushrooms, cream cheese and gravy mix to skillet; cook and stir until well blended. Add beef mixture to Dutch oven; stir until noodles are coated.

5 Bake 30 minutes or until heated through.

CAJUN-STYLE BEEF AND BEANS

MAKES 6 SERVINGS

1 pound ground beef

¾ cup chopped onion

2½ cups cooked brown rice

1 can (about 15 ounces) kidney beans, rinsed and drained

1 can (about 14 ounces) stewed tomatoes

2 teaspoons Cajun seasoning

¾ cup (3 ounces) shredded Cheddar cheese

1 Preheat oven to 350°F.

2 Brown beef in large skillet over medium-high heat 6 to 8 minutes, stirring to break up meat. Drain fat. Add onion; cook and stir 3 minutes or until translucent.

3 Combine beef mixture, rice, beans, tomatoes and Cajun seasoning in 2- to 2½-quart casserole; mix well.

4 Cover and bake 25 to 30 minutes, stirring once. Sprinkle with cheese; cover and let stand 5 minutes before serving.

TIP: To make your own Cajun seasoning, combine 5 tablespoons ground red pepper, 3 tablespoons black pepper, 3 tablespoons onion powder, 3 tablespoons garlic powder, 3 tablespoons chili powder, 1 tablespoon dried thyme, 1 tablespoon dried basil and 1 tablespoon ground bay leaf in a medium bowl; mix well. If desired, stir in ½ cup salt. Store in a tightly sealed container.

PIZZA CASSEROLE

MAKES 6 SERVINGS

2 cups uncooked rotini
   or other spiral pasta

1½ pounds ground beef

1 medium onion,
   chopped

   Salt and black pepper

1 can (about 15 ounces)
   pizza sauce

1 can (8 ounces)
   tomato sauce

1 can (6 ounces)
   tomato paste

½ teaspoon sugar

½ teaspoon garlic salt

½ teaspoon dried
   oregano

2 cups (8 ounces)
   shredded mozzarella
   cheese

12 to 15 slices pepperoni

1 Preheat oven to 350°F.

2 Cook pasta according to package directions;
   drain well.

3 Meanwhile, brown beef and onion in large
   skillet over medium-high heat 6 to 8 minutes,
   stirring to break up meat. Drain fat. Season
   with salt and pepper.

4 Combine pasta, pizza sauce, tomato sauce,
   tomato paste, sugar, garlic salt and oregano
   in large bowl; mix well. Add beef mixture;
   stir until blended.

5 Spread half of mixture in ovenproof skillet
   or 3-quart casserole; top with 1 cup cheese.
   Repeat layers. Top with pepperoni slices.

6 Bake 25 to 30 minutes or until heated through
   and cheese is melted.

FIESTA BEEF ENCHILADAS

MAKES 6 SERVINGS

1 pound ground beef

½ cup sliced green onions

2 teaspoons minced garlic

1½ cups chopped tomatoes, divided

1 cup cooked white or brown rice

1 cup (4 ounces) shredded Mexican cheese blend or Cheddar cheese, divided

¾ cup frozen corn, thawed

½ cup salsa or picante sauce

12 (6- to 7-inch) corn tortillas

1 can (10 ounces) enchilada sauce

1 cup shredded romaine lettuce

1 Preheat oven to 375°F. Spray 13×9-inch baking dish with nonstick cooking spray.

2 Brown beef in large skillet over medium-high heat 6 to 8 minutes, stirring to break up meat. Drain fat. Add green onions and garlic; cook and stir 2 minutes.

3 Remove from heat; stir in 1 cup tomatoes, rice, ½ cup cheese, corn and salsa.

4 Spoon beef mixture down center of tortillas. Roll up; place seam side down in prepared baking dish. Spoon enchilada sauce evenly over enchiladas.

5 Cover and bake 20 minutes or until heated through. Sprinkle with remaining ½ cup cheese; bake, uncovered, 5 minutes or until cheese is melted. Top with lettuce and remaining ½ cup tomatoes.

NO-CHOP PASTITSIO

MAKES 6 SERVINGS

- 1 pound ground beef or ground lamb
- 1½ cups mild picante sauce
- 1 can (8 ounces) tomato sauce
- 1 tablespoon sugar
- ½ teaspoon ground allspice
- ½ teaspoon ground cinnamon
- ¼ teaspoon ground nutmeg, divided
- 8 ounces uncooked elbow macaroni
- 3 tablespoons butter
- 3 tablespoons all-purpose flour
- 1½ cups milk
- ½ teaspoon salt
- ¼ teaspoon black pepper
- 2 eggs, beaten
- ½ cup grated Parmesan cheese

1 Preheat oven to 350°F. Spray 9-inch square baking dish with nonstick cooking spray.

2 Brown beef in large skillet over medium-high heat 6 to 8 minutes, stirring to break up meat. Drain fat. Add picante sauce, tomato sauce, sugar, allspice, cinnamon and ⅛ teaspoon nutmeg; bring to a boil. Reduce heat to medium-low; cook 10 minutes, stirring frequently.

3 Meanwhile, cook macaroni according to package directions; drain well. Place in prepared baking dish.

4 Melt butter in medium saucepan over medium heat. Add flour; stir until smooth. Add milk, salt and pepper; cook and stir until thickened. Remove from heat. Add about ½ cup white sauce to eggs in small bowl; stir until blended. Add egg mixture to remaining white sauce in saucepan, stirring constantly. Stir in cheese.

5 Add about ½ cup white sauce to macaroni; toss to coat. Spread meat sauce over macaroni. Top with remaining white sauce; sprinkle with remaining ⅛ teaspoon nutmeg.

6 Bake, uncovered, 30 to 40 minutes or until knife inserted into center comes out clean. Let stand 15 to 20 minutes before serving.

SPINACH-POTATO BAKE

MAKES 6 SERVINGS

1 pound ground beef

1 small onion, chopped

½ cup sliced mushrooms

2 cloves garlic, minced

1 package (10 ounces) frozen chopped spinach, thawed and squeezed dry

½ teaspoon ground nutmeg

1 pound russet potatoes, peeled, cooked and mashed

¼ cup sour cream

¼ cup milk

Salt and black pepper

½ cup (2 ounces) shredded Cheddar cheese

1 Preheat oven to 400°F. Spray 9-inch square baking dish with nonstick cooking spray.

2 Brown beef in large skillet over medium-high heat 6 to 8 minutes, stirring to break up meat. Drain all but 1 tablespoon fat. Add onion, mushrooms and garlic to skillet; cook and stir until tender. Add spinach and nutmeg; cook until heated through, stirring occasionally.

3 Combine potatoes, sour cream and milk in medium bowl; mix well. Add to beef mixture; season with salt and pepper. Spoon into prepared baking dish; sprinkle with cheese.

4 Bake 15 to 20 minutes or until slightly puffed and cheese is melted.

MEXICAN LASAGNA

MAKES 4 SERVINGS

1 pound ground beef

1 package (1½ ounces) taco seasoning mix

1 can (about 14 ounces) Mexican-style diced tomatoes

1½ teaspoons chili powder

1 teaspoon ground cumin

½ teaspoon salt

½ teaspoon red pepper flakes

2 cups (16 ounces) sour cream

1 can (4 ounces) diced mild green chiles, drained

6 green onions, chopped

6 to 7 (8-inch) flour tortillas

1 can (15 ounces) corn, drained

2 cups (8 ounces) shredded Cheddar cheese

1 Preheat oven to 350°F. Spray 13×9-inch baking dish with nonstick cooking spray.

2 Brown beef with taco seasoning mix in large skillet over medium-high heat 6 to 8 minutes, stirring to break up meat. Drain fat.

3 Combine tomatoes, chili powder, cumin, salt and red pepper flakes in medium bowl. Combine sour cream, chiles and green onions in small bowl; mix well.

4 Layer one third of tomato mixture, 2 tortillas, one third of sour cream mixture, one third of meat mixture, one third of corn and one third of cheese in prepared baking dish. Repeat layers twice.

5 Bake 35 minutes or until bubbly. Let stand 15 minutes before serving.

SPICY MANICOTTI

MAKES 8 SERVINGS

3 cups ricotta cheese

1 cup grated Parmesan cheese, divided

2 eggs, lightly beaten

2½ tablespoons chopped fresh parsley

1 teaspoon Italian seasoning

½ teaspoon garlic powder

½ teaspoon salt

½ teaspoon black pepper

1 pound ground beef or Italian sausage

1 can (28 ounces) crushed tomatoes

1 jar (26 ounces) marinara sauce

½ teaspoon red pepper flakes

8 ounces uncooked manicotti shells

1 Preheat oven to 375°F. Spray 13×9-inch baking dish with nonstick cooking spray.

2 For filling, combine ricotta, ¾ cup Parmesan, eggs, parsley, Italian seasoning, garlic powder, salt and black pepper in medium bowl; mix well.

3 Brown beef in large skillet over medium-high heat 6 to 8 minutes, stirring to separate meat. Drain fat.

4 Add tomatoes, marinara sauce and red pepper flakes to skillet; bring to a boil over high heat. Reduce heat to low; cook 10 minutes, stirring occasionally. Spread about one third of sauce in prepared baking dish.

5 Stuff each manicotti shell with about ½ cup filling. Arrange filled shells in sauce in baking dish; top with remaining sauce.

6 Cover and bake 50 minutes to 1 hour or until shells are tender. Let stand 5 minutes before serving. Sprinkle with remaining ¼ cup Parmesan.

BEEF POT PIE
WITH BEER BISCUITS

MAKES 6 SERVINGS

4 slices bacon, coarsely chopped

2½ pounds boneless beef chuck roast, cut into 1-inch pieces

2¼ teaspoons salt, divided

½ teaspoon black pepper

1 large onion, chopped

3 carrots, cut into ½-inch slices

3 stalks celery, cut into ½-inch pieces

2 cloves garlic, minced

2⅓ cups plus 1 tablespoon all-purpose flour, divided

1 can (about 14 ounces) beef broth

2 tablespoons Worcestershire sauce

1 teaspoon dried thyme

2½ teaspoons baking powder

6 tablespoons butter, cut into ½-inch cubes

¾ cup lager

1 Preheat oven to 350°F. Cook bacon in Dutch oven over medium heat until crisp and browned. Remove to paper towel-lined plate. Drain all but 2 tablespoons drippings.

2 Season beef with 1½ teaspoons salt and pepper; add to Dutch oven in batches. Cook and stir over medium-high heat 5 minutes or until browned. Remove to plate with slotted spoon; reserve fat in Dutch oven.

3 Add onion, carrots, celery and garlic to Dutch oven; cook and stir over medium heat 5 minutes or until vegetables are tender. Sprinkle with ⅓ cup plus 1 tablespoon flour; stir until blended. Stir in bacon, beef, broth, Worcestershire sauce and thyme; bring to a boil.

4 Cover and bake 1½ hours or until beef is almost tender.

5 Meanwhile, for biscuits, whisk remaining 2 cups flour, baking powder and remaining ¾ teaspoon salt in medium bowl. Cut in butter with pastry blender or two knives until mixture resembles coarse crumbs. Stir in enough lager to make soft dough. Turn dough out onto lightly floured surface; roll into 9×6-inch rectangle about ½ inch thick. Cut into six 3-inch square biscuits.

6 Remove Dutch oven from oven. *Increase oven temperature to 400°F.* Arrange biscuits over stew, overlapping if necessary. Bake 20 minutes or until biscuits are light golden brown.

BEEF, BEAN AND PASTA CASSEROLE

MAKES 6 SERVINGS

2¾ cups uncooked whole wheat rigatoni pasta

1 pound ground beef

1 medium onion, diced

2 cloves garlic, minced

1 can (about 15 ounces) cannellini beans, rinsed and drained

1 can (about 14 ounces) diced tomatoes, drained

1 can (8 ounces) tomato sauce

2 teaspoons Italian seasoning

¾ teaspoon salt

¼ teaspoon black pepper

1 cup finely shredded Parmesan cheese

1 cup (4 ounces) shredded mozzarella cheese

1 Preheat oven to 350°F. Spray 11×7-inch baking dish with nonstick cooking spray.

2 Cook pasta according to package directions; drain well.

3 Meanwhile, combine beef, onion and garlic in large nonstick skillet; cook over medium-high heat 6 to 8 minutes, stirring to break up meat. Drain fat. Stir in beans, tomatoes, tomato sauce, Italian seasoning, salt and pepper; cook 3 minutes.

4 Remove skillet from heat; stir in pasta and Parmesan. Transfer to prepared baking dish; sprinkle with mozzarella.

5 Bake 20 minutes or until bubbly and cheeses are melted.

VARIATIONS: Any short-shape pasta can be used in this recipe. Red kidney beans can be used in place of the cannellini beans.

TACO SALAD CASSEROLE

MAKES 6 TO 8 SERVINGS

1 pound ground beef

1 cup chopped onion

1 can (15 ounces) chili with beans

1 can (about 14 ounces) diced tomatoes

1 can (4 ounces) diced mild green chiles, undrained

1 package (1½ ounces) taco seasoning mix

1 bag (12 ounces) nacho-flavor tortilla chips, crushed

2 cups (8 ounces) shredded Cheddar cheese

2 cups (8 ounces) shredded mozzarella cheese

3 to 4 cups shredded lettuce

1 jar (8 ounces) prepared taco sauce

½ cup sour cream

1 Preheat oven to 350°F.

2 Brown beef and onion in large skillet over medium-high heat 6 to 8 minutes, stirring to break up meat. Drain fat. Add chili with beans, tomatoes, green chiles and taco seasoning mix; cook and stir until heated through.

3 Spread half of crushed tortilla chips in 2½-quart casserole. Pour meat mixture over chips; top with cheeses and remaining chips.

4 Bake 30 to 40 minutes or until hot and bubbly. Serve over lettuce; top with taco sauce and sour cream.

PORK

SAUSAGE, POTATO AND APPLE BAKE

MAKES 6 SERVINGS

- 3 tablespoons packed brown sugar
- 1 tablespoon dried thyme
- 1 tablespoon dried oregano
- ¼ cup dry white wine or apple cider
- 2 tablespoons cider vinegar
- 2 sweet potatoes (1½ to 2 pounds), peeled
- 2 apples, such as Fuji or McIntosh, peeled
- 1 white onion
- 1 red bell pepper
- 1 yellow bell pepper
- ½ cup golden raisins
- 1½ pounds smoked sausage, such as kielbasa or Polish sausage, cut diagonally into ¼-inch slices

1 Preheat oven to 450°F. Spray 2-quart casserole or 13×9-inch baking dish with nonstick cooking spray.

2 Combine brown sugar, thyme and oregano in large bowl. Stir in white wine and vinegar until brown sugar is dissolved.

3 Spiral sweet potatoes, apples and onion with thick spiral blade. Spiral bell peppers with spiral slicing blade.* Cut vegetables into desired lengths. Add vegetables and raisins to brown sugar mixture; toss to coat.

4 Transfer vegetables to prepared casserole with tongs or slotted spoon. Stir in sausage; drizzle with remaining brown sugar mixture.

5 Bake 20 minutes or until vegetables are tender.

*If you don't have a spiralizer, cut the vegetables and apples into thin strips.

HAM JAMBALAYA

MAKES 6 TO 8 SERVINGS

- 2 tablespoons butter
- 1 onion, chopped
- ½ cup thinly sliced celery
- ½ red bell pepper, diced
- 2 cloves garlic, minced
- 1 jar (about 16 ounces) medium salsa
- 2 cups cubed cooked ham
- 1 cup uncooked long grain rice
- 1 cup water
- ⅔ cup vegetable broth
- 3 teaspoons prepared horseradish
- 2 teaspoons honey
- ¼ to ½ teaspoon hot pepper sauce
- 1½ pounds medium or large raw shrimp, peeled and deveined
- 1 tablespoon chopped fresh mint

1 Preheat oven to 350°F.

2 Melt butter in Dutch oven over medium heat. Add onion, celery, bell pepper and garlic; cook and stir 4 minutes or until tender. Stir in salsa, ham, rice, water, broth, horseradish, honey and hot pepper sauce; mix well.

3 Cover and bake 40 minutes or until rice is almost tender.

4 Stir in shrimp and mint; cover and bake 10 to 15 minutes or until shrimp are pink and opaque.

HEARTY NOODLE CASSEROLE

MAKES 4 TO 6 SERVINGS

1 pound Italian sausage, casings removed

1 jar (26 ounces) pasta sauce

2 cups (16 ounces) ricotta or cottage cheese

1 package (12 ounces) extra wide egg noodles, cooked and drained

2 cups (8 ounces) shredded mozzarella cheese

1 can (4 ounces) sliced mushrooms, drained

½ cup chopped green bell pepper

1 Preheat oven to 350°F.

2 Brown sausage in large skillet over medium-high heat 6 to 8 minutes, stirring to break up meat. Drain fat.

3 Combine sausage, pasta sauce, ricotta, noodles, 1 cup mozzarella, mushrooms and bell pepper in large bowl; mix gently. Transfer to 13×9-inch or 3-quart baking dish; top with remaining 1 cup mozzarella.

4 Bake 25 minutes or until heated through.

HAM AND CHEESE PUFF PIE

MAKES 4 TO 6 SERVINGS

2 cups (about 1 pound) diced cooked ham

1 package (10 ounces) frozen chopped spinach, thawed and squeezed dry

½ cup diced red bell pepper

4 green onions, sliced

3 eggs

¾ cup all-purpose flour

¾ cup (3 ounces) shredded Swiss cheese

¾ cup milk

1 tablespoon prepared mustard

1 teaspoon grated lemon peel

1 teaspoon dried dill weed

½ teaspoon garlic salt

½ teaspoon black pepper

Fresh dill sprigs and lemon slices (optional)

1 Preheat oven to 425°F. Spray 2-quart round baking dish with nonstick cooking spray.

2 Combine ham, spinach, bell pepper and green onions in prepared baking dish; mix well.

3 Beat eggs in medium bowl. Add flour, cheese, milk, mustard, lemon peel, dill weed, garlic salt and black pepper; beat until well blended. Pour over ham mixture.

4 Bake 30 to 35 minutes or until puffed and browned. Garnish as desired.

TUSCAN BAKED RIGATONI

MAKES 6 TO 8 SERVINGS

1 pound bulk Italian sausage

1 package (16 ounces) rigatoni pasta, cooked, drained and kept warm

2 cups (8 ounces) shredded fontina cheese

2 tablespoons olive oil

2 bulbs fennel, thinly sliced

4 cloves garlic, minced

1 can (28 ounces) crushed tomatoes

1 cup whipping cream

1 teaspoon salt

1 teaspoon black pepper

8 cups packed fresh spinach

1 can (about 15 ounces) cannellini beans, rinsed and drained

2 tablespoons pine nuts

½ cup grated Parmesan cheese

1 Preheat oven to 350°F. Spray 4-quart casserole with nonstick cooking spray.

2 Brown sausage in large skillet over medium-high heat, stirring to break up meat. Drain fat. Transfer to large bowl. Add rigatoni and fontina cheese; mix well.

3 Heat oil in same skillet. Add fennel and garlic; cook and stir over medium heat 3 minutes or until fennel is tender. Add tomatoes, cream, salt and pepper; cook and stir until slightly thickened. Stir in spinach, beans and pine nuts; cook until heated through.

4 Pour sauce mixture over pasta mixture; toss to coat. Transfer to prepared casserole; sprinkle with Parmesan.

5 Bake 30 minutes or until bubbly and heated through.

SAUSAGE AND POLENTA CASSEROLE

MAKES 4 SERVINGS

1 tablespoon olive oil

1 cup chopped mushrooms

1 red bell pepper, chopped

1 onion, diced

1 pound bulk Italian sausage

1 jar (28 to 30 ounces) meatless pasta sauce

1 roll (16 to 18 ounces) polenta

¼ cup shredded Parmesan cheese

1 Preheat oven to 350°F. Spray 8-inch square baking dish with nonstick cooking spray.

2 Heat oil in large skillet over medium heat. Add mushrooms, bell pepper and onion; cook and stir 5 minutes or until vegetables are tender. Add sausage; cook and stir until sausage is browned, breaking into small pieces with spoon. Drain fat. Stir in pasta sauce; cook 5 minutes.

3 Cut polenta crosswise into 9 slices; arrange in prepared baking dish. Top with sausage mixture.

4 Bake 15 minutes or until heated through. Sprinkle with cheese.

PORK AND CORN BREAD STUFFING BAKE

MAKES 4 SERVINGS

½ teaspoon paprika

¼ teaspoon salt

¼ teaspoon garlic powder

¼ teaspoon black pepper

4 bone-in pork chops (about 1¾ pounds)

2 tablespoons butter

1½ cups chopped onions

¾ cup thinly sliced celery

¾ cup matchstick carrots*

¼ cup chopped fresh Italian parsley

1 can (about 14 ounces) chicken broth

4 cups corn bread stuffing mix

Matchstick carrots (sometimes called shredded carrots) can be found near other prepared vegetables in the supermarket produce section.

1 Preheat oven to 350°F. Spray 13×9-inch baking dish with nonstick cooking spray.

2 Combine paprika, salt, garlic powder and pepper in small bowl; sprinkle over both sides of pork chops.

3 Melt butter in large skillet over medium-high heat. Add pork; cook 4 minutes or just until browned, turning once. Remove to plate.

4 Add onions, celery, carrots and parsley to same skillet; cook and stir 4 minutes or until onions are translucent. Stir in broth; bring to a boil. Remove from heat; add stuffing mix and fluff with fork. Transfer to prepared baking dish; top with pork chops.

5 Cover and bake 25 minutes or until pork is barely pink in center.

VARIATION: For a one-dish meal, use an ovenproof skillet. Place browned pork chops on mixture in skillet; cover and bake as directed.

CARIBBEAN BLACK BEAN CASSEROLE WITH SPICY MANGO SALSA

MAKES 6 SERVINGS

2 cups chicken broth

1 cup uncooked basmati rice

2 tablespoons olive oil, divided

½ pound Spanish-style chorizo sausage links

1 cup chopped red bell pepper

2 cloves garlic, minced

3 cups canned black beans, rinsed and drained

½ cup chopped fresh cilantro

2 small mangoes

1 cup chopped red onion

2 tablespoons honey

2 tablespoons white wine vinegar

1 teaspoon curry powder

½ teaspoon salt

½ teaspoon ground red pepper

1 Bring broth to a boil in medium saucepan over high heat; stir in rice. Reduce heat to low; cover and simmer 20 minutes or until liquid is absorbed and rice is tender.

2 Preheat oven to 350°F. Spray 1½-quart baking dish with nonstick cooking spray.

3 Heat 1 tablespoon oil in large skillet over medium heat. Add sausage; cook 8 to 10 minutes until browned and cooked through, turning occasionally. Remove to cutting board; cut sausage diagonally into 1-inch slices. Drain fat from skillet.

4 Add remaining 1 tablespoon oil to same skillet; heat over medium-high heat. Add bell pepper; cook and stir until tender. Add garlic; cook and stir 30 seconds. Remove from heat; stir in beans, sausage, rice and cilantro. Transfer to prepared baking dish; cover with foil.

5 Bake 30 minutes or until heated through.

6 Meanwhile, peel mangoes and chop enough flesh to measure 3 cups. Combine mangoes, red onion, honey, vinegar, curry power, salt and ground red pepper in large bowl; mix well. Serve with casserole.

HAM AND CHEESE GRITS SOUFFLÉ

MAKES 4 TO 6 SERVINGS

3 cups water

¾ cup quick-cooking grits

½ teaspoon salt

½ cup (2 ounces) shredded mozzarella cheese

2 ounces ham, finely chopped

2 tablespoons minced fresh chives

2 eggs, separated

Dash hot pepper sauce

1 Preheat oven to 375°F. Spray 1½-quart soufflé dish or deep round casserole with nonstick cooking spray.

2 Bring water to a boil in medium saucepan over medium heat; stir in grits and salt. Cook and stir 5 minutes or until thickened. Stir in cheese, ham, chives, egg yolks and hot pepper sauce; mix well.

3 Beat egg whites in small bowl with electric mixer at high speed until stiff peaks form. Fold into grits mixture; spoon into prepared soufflé dish.

4 Bake 30 minutes or until puffed and golden. Serve immediately.

BAKED PASTA AND CHEESE SUPREME

MAKES 4 SERVINGS

8 ounces uncooked fusilli pasta or other corkscrew-shaped pasta

12 slices bacon, chopped

½ medium onion, chopped

2 cloves garlic, minced

2 teaspoons dried oregano, divided

1 can (8 ounces) tomato sauce

1 teaspoon hot pepper sauce (optional)

1½ cups (6 ounces) shredded Cheddar or Colby cheese

½ cup fresh bread crumbs (from 1 slice of white bread)

1 tablespoon butter, melted

1 Preheat oven to 400°F.

2 Cook pasta according to package directions; drain well.

3 Meanwhile, cook bacon in large ovenproof skillet over medium heat until crisp. Drain on paper towel-lined plate.

4 Add onion, garlic and 1 teaspoon oregano to skillet; cook and stir 3 minutes or until onion is translucent. Stir in tomato sauce and hot pepper sauce, if desired. Add pasta and cheese; stir to coat.

5 Combine bacon, bread crumbs, remaining 1 teaspoon oregano and butter in small bowl; sprinkle over pasta mixture.

6 Bake 10 to 15 minutes or until hot and bubbly.

POTATO AND PORK FRITTATA

MAKES 4 SERVINGS

12 ounces (about 3 cups)
   frozen hash brown
   potatoes

 1 teaspoon Cajun
   seasoning

 3 eggs

 3 egg whites

¼ cup milk

 1 teaspoon salt

 1 teaspoon dry mustard

¼ teaspoon black
   pepper

10 ounces (about
   3 cups) frozen
   stir-fry vegetable
   blend

⅓ cup water

¾ cup chopped
   cooked pork

½ cup (2 ounces)
   shredded Cheddar
   cheese

1 Preheat oven to 400°F. Spray baking sheet with nonstick cooking spray. Spread potatoes on prepared baking sheet; sprinkle with Cajun seasoning. Bake 15 minutes or until hot. *Reduce oven temperature to 350°F.*

2 Beat eggs, egg whites, milk, salt, mustard and pepper in small bowl until well blended.

3 Combine vegetables and water in medium ovenproof nonstick skillet; cook over medium heat 5 minutes or until vegetables are crisp-tender. Drain vegetables.

4 Add potatoes and pork to vegetables in skillet; stir gently. Add egg mixture; sprinkle with cheese. Cook over medium heat 5 minutes.

5 Bake 5 minutes or until egg mixture is set and cheese is melted. Cut into wedges.

CHEESY ITALIAN NOODLE BAKE

MAKES 8 TO 10 SERVINGS

4 packages (3 ounces each) ramen noodles, any flavor*

1 pound sweet Italian sausage, casings removed

2 teaspoons olive oil

1 cup diced onion

1 cup diced red bell pepper

1 teaspoon minced garlic

1 can (about 15 ounces) tomato sauce

½ cup thinly sliced fresh basil

2 cups (8 ounces) shredded mozzarella cheese

Discard seasoning packets.

1 Preheat oven to 400°F. Spray 13×9-inch baking dish with nonstick cooking spray.

2 Cook noodles according to package directions; drain well. Transfer to large bowl.

3 Brown sausage in large skillet over medium-high heat 8 minutes, stirring to break up meat. Drain on paper towel-lined plate. Add to bowl with noodles.

4 Heat oil in same skillet. Add onion and bell pepper; cook and stir 6 minutes or until softened. Add garlic; cook and stir 30 seconds. Add vegetable mixture, tomato sauce and basil to bowl with noodles; stir to coat. Transfer to prepared baking dish; sprinkle with cheese.

5 Bake 25 to 30 minutes or until bubbly and cheese is melted. Let stand 5 minutes before serving.

SAVORY LENTIL CASSEROLE

MAKES 4 SERVINGS

1¼ cups dried brown or green lentils, rinsed and sorted

2 tablespoons olive oil

1 large onion, chopped

3 cloves garlic, minced

8 ounces fresh shiitake or button mushrooms, sliced

2 tablespoons all-purpose flour

1½ cups beef broth

4 ounces Canadian bacon, minced

1 tablespoon Worcestershire sauce

1 tablespoon balsamic vinegar

½ teaspoon salt

½ teaspoon black pepper

½ cup grated Parmesan cheese

2 to 3 plum tomatoes, seeded and chopped

Fresh Italian parsley (optional)

1 Preheat oven to 400°F. Spray 1½-quart baking dish with nonstick cooking spray.

2 Place lentils in medium saucepan; add water to cover by 1 inch. Bring to a boil over high heat. Reduce heat to low; cover and cook 20 to 25 minutes or just until lentils are tender. Drain lentils.

3 Meanwhile, heat oil in large skillet over medium heat. Add onion and garlic; cook and stir 5 minutes. Add mushrooms; cook and stir 10 minutes or until liquid is evaporated and mushrooms are tender.

4 Sprinkle flour over mushroom mixture; cook and stir 1 minute. Add broth, Canadian bacon, Worcestershire sauce, vinegar, salt and pepper; cook and stir until mixture is thick and bubbly. Stir in lentils. Transfer to prepared baking dish; sprinkle with cheese.

5 Bake 20 minutes. Sprinkle tomatoes over casserole just before serving. Garnish with parsley.

POULTRY

SPLIT-BISCUIT CHICKEN PIE

MAKES 4 TO 5 SERVINGS

⅓ cup butter

⅓ cup all-purpose flour

2½ cups whole milk

1 tablespoon chicken bouillon granules

½ teaspoon dried thyme

½ teaspoon black pepper

4 cups diced cooked chicken

2 jars (4 ounces each) diced pimientos

1 cup frozen green peas, thawed

1 package (6 ounces) refrigerated biscuit dough

1 Preheat oven to 350°F. Spray 2-quart casserole or 12×8-inch baking dish with nonstick cooking spray.

2 Melt butter in large skillet over medium heat. Add flour; stir until smooth. Add milk, bouillon, thyme and pepper; stir until well blended. Cook and stir until thickened. Remove from heat; stir in chicken, pimientos and peas. Transfer to prepared casserole.

3 Bake 30 minutes. Meanwhile, bake biscuits according to package directions.

4 Split biscuits in half; arrange cut sides down over chicken mixture. Bake 3 minutes or until biscuits are heated through.

VARIATIONS: For a one-dish meal, use an ovenproof skillet. Use whole biscuits instead of halves.

CAJUN CHICKEN AND RICE

MAKES 6 SERVINGS

- 4 chicken drumsticks, skin removed
- 4 chicken thighs, skin removed
- 2 teaspoons Cajun seasoning
- ¾ teaspoon salt
- 2 tablespoons vegetable oil
- 1 can (about 14 ounces) chicken broth
- 1 cup uncooked rice
- 1 medium green bell pepper, coarsely chopped
- 1 medium red bell pepper, coarsely chopped
- ½ cup finely chopped green onions
- 2 cloves garlic, minced
- ½ teaspoon dried thyme
- ¼ teaspoon ground turmeric

1 Preheat oven to 350°F. Spray 13×9-inch baking dish with nonstick cooking spray.

2 Pat chicken dry; sprinkle both sides with Cajun seasoning and salt. Heat oil in large skillet over medium-high heat. Add chicken; cook 8 to 10 minutes or until browned on all sides. Remove to plate.

3 Add broth to skillet; bring to a boil, scraping up any browned bits from bottom of skillet. Add rice, bell peppers, green onions, garlic, thyme and turmeric; mix well. Transfer to prepared baking dish; top with chicken.

4 Cover and bake 1 hour or until chicken is cooked through (165°F).

VARIATION: For a one-dish meal, use an ovenproof skillet. Place browned chicken over rice mixture in skillet, then cover and bake as directed.

TURKEY MEATBALL AND OLIVE CASSEROLE

MAKES 6 TO 8 SERVINGS

2 cups uncooked rotini pasta

½ pound ground turkey

½ cup seasoned dry bread crumbs, divided

1 egg, lightly beaten

2 teaspoons dried minced onion

2 teaspoons Worcestershire sauce

½ teaspoon Italian seasoning

½ teaspoon salt

⅛ teaspoon black pepper

1 tablespoon vegetable oil

1 can (10¾ ounces) condensed cream of celery soup, undiluted

½ cup plain yogurt

¾ cup pimiento-stuffed green olives, sliced

1 tablespoon butter, melted

Paprika (optional)

1 Preheat oven to 350°F. Spray 2-quart round casserole with nonstick cooking spray.

2 Cook pasta according to package directions until almost tender; drain well.

3 Meanwhile, combine turkey, ¼ cup bread crumbs, egg, onion, Worcestershire sauce, Italian seasoning, salt and pepper in medium bowl. Shape mixture into ½-inch meatballs.

4 Heat oil in large skillet over high heat. Add meatballs in single layer; cook until lightly browned on all sides. Drain on paper towel-lined plate.

5 Combine soup and yogurt in large bowl; mix well. Add pasta, meatballs and olives; stir gently to coat. Transfer to prepared casserole.

6 Combine remaining ¼ cup bread crumbs and butter in small bowl; sprinkle over casserole. Sprinkle lightly with paprika, if desired.

7 Cover and bake 30 minutes. Uncover; bake 12 minutes or until meatballs are cooked through and casserole is bubbly.

EASY CHICKEN CHALUPAS

MAKES 6 SERVINGS

1 rotisserie chicken
   (about 2 pounds)

8 (8-inch) flour tortillas

2 cups (8 ounces)
   shredded Cheddar
   cheese

1 cup mild green salsa

1 cup mild red salsa

1 Preheat oven to 350°F. Spray 13×9-inch baking dish with nonstick cooking spray.

2 Shred chicken; discard skin and bones.

3 Place 2 tortillas in prepared baking dish, overlapping slightly. Layer tortillas with ¾ cup chicken, ½ cup cheese and ¼ cup of each salsa. Repeat layers three times.

4 Bake 25 minutes or until bubbly and heated through.

TIP: Serve with toppings such as sour cream, chopped fresh cilantro, sliced black olives, sliced green onions and sliced avocado.

PIZZA CHICKEN BAKE

MAKES 4 SERVINGS

3½ cups uncooked bowtie pasta

1 tablespoon vegetable oil

1 cup sliced mushrooms

1 jar (26 ounces) herb-flavored pasta sauce

1 teaspoon pizza seasoning blend

3 boneless skinless chicken breasts (about 12 ounces), quartered

1 cup (4 ounces) shredded mozzarella cheese

1 Preheat oven to 350°F. Spray 2-quart round casserole with nonstick cooking spray.

2 Cook pasta according to package directions until al dente; drain and place in prepared casserole.

3 Meanwhile, heat oil in large skillet over medium-high heat. Add mushrooms; cook and stir 5 minutes. Remove from heat; stir in pasta sauce and pizza seasoning.

4 Pour half of pasta sauce mixture over pasta; stir gently to coat. Top with chicken and remaining pasta sauce mixture.

5 Cover and bake 50 minutes or until chicken is no longer pink in center. Remove from oven; sprinkle with cheese. Cover and let stand 5 minutes before serving.

TIP: Serve with grated Parmesan cheese and red pepper flakes so that everyone can add their own pizza seasonings.

WILD RICE AND CHICKEN CASSEROLE

MAKES 4 TO 6 SERVINGS

1 package (6 ounces) long grain and wild rice mix

2 tablespoons butter

½ cup chopped onion

½ cup chopped celery

2 cups cubed cooked chicken

1 can (10¾ ounces) condensed cream of mushroom soup, undiluted

½ cup sour cream

⅓ cup dry white wine

½ teaspoon curry powder

1 Preheat oven to 350°F.

2 Prepare rice mix according to package directions.

3 Meanwhile, melt butter in large skillet over medium heat. Add onion and celery; cook and stir until tender. Add rice, chicken, soup, sour cream, wine and curry powder; mix well. Transfer to 2-quart casserole.

4 Bake 40 minutes or until heated through.

CHICKEN CHILAQUILES

MAKES 6 TO 8 SERVINGS

12 (6- or 7-inch) corn tortillas

1 tablespoon vegetable oil

2 cups shredded cooked chicken

4½ cups chipotle salsa

6 eggs, beaten

1 cup (4 ounces) shredded Chihuahua or Manchego cheese

½ cup finely crumbled queso añejo or feta cheese

⅓ cup crema mexicana or crème fraîche

1 Preheat oven to 375°F. Spray 13×9-inch baking dish with nonstick cooking spray.

2 Place tortillas in single stack on cutting board; cut into ½-inch-wide strips. Heat half of oil in large skillet over medium-high heat until shimmering. Add half of tortilla strips; cook until golden brown, stirring frequently to separate strips. Transfer to prepared baking dish with slotted spoon. Add remaining oil to skillet, if necessary; repeat with remaining tortilla strips.

3 Add chicken to baking dish. Pour salsa over tortilla strips and chicken; toss gently to coat. Stir in eggs.

4 Cover and bake 35 minutes or until tortillas are soft but not soggy and casserole is heated through. Sprinkle with Chihuahua cheese; bake, uncovered, 5 to 10 minutes or until cheese is melted and top is beginning to brown. Let stand 5 minutes before serving. Sprinkle with queso añejo; drizzle with crema mexicana.

TIP: Crema mexicana is a dairy product similar to sour cream or crème fraîche. Crema mexicana is sweeter and creamier than crème fraîche, but it has a slightly bolder flavor than sour cream.

MOM'S BEST CHICKEN TETRAZZINI

MAKES 6 SERVINGS

8 ounces uncooked thin noodles or vermicelli pasta

2 tablespoons butter

8 ounces mushrooms, sliced

¼ cup chopped green onions

1 can (about 14 ounces) chicken broth

1 cup half-and-half, divided

2 tablespoons dry sherry

¼ cup all-purpose flour

½ teaspoon salt

¼ teaspoon ground nutmeg

⅛ teaspoon white pepper

1 jar (2 ounces) chopped pimientos, drained

½ cup grated Parmesan cheese, divided

½ cup sour cream

2 cups cubed cooked chicken

1 Preheat oven to 350°F. Spray 1½-quart casserole with nonstick cooking spray.

2 Cook noodles according to package directions; drain well.

3 Meanwhile, melt butter in large nonstick skillet over medium-high heat. Add mushrooms and green onions; cook and stir until green onions are tender. Stir in broth, ½ cup half-and-half and sherry.

4 Pour remaining ½ cup half-and-half into small jar with tight-fitting lid. Add flour, salt, nutmeg and pepper; shake until well blended. Slowly stir flour mixture into skillet. Bring to a boil; cook and stir 1 minute. Reduce heat to low; stir in pimientos, ¼ cup cheese and sour cream. Add chicken and noodles; mix well. Transfer to prepared casserole; sprinkle with remaining ¼ cup cheese.

5 Bake 30 to 35 minutes or until heated through.

CARMEL CHICKEN FRESCO BAKE

MAKES 8 SERVINGS

4 cups broccoli florets

4 tablespoons butter, divided

12 ounces baby portobello mushrooms, sliced

3 shallots, diced

1 can (14 ounces) artichoke hearts, rinsed, drained and quartered

¼ cup all-purpose flour

2½ cups chicken broth

1 teaspoon Dijon mustard

½ teaspoon salt

½ teaspoon dried tarragon

½ teaspoon black pepper

1 cup (4 ounces) shredded Emmentaler cheese

2 pounds boneless skinless chicken breasts, cooked and cut into 1½-inch pieces

¼ cup grated Asiago cheese

1 Preheat oven to 350°F. Spray 4-quart baking dish with nonstick cooking spray.

2 Steam broccoli about 6 minutes or until tender; rinse and drain under cold water. Place in large bowl.

3 Melt 1 tablespoon butter in medium skillet over medium heat. Add mushrooms and shallots; cook and stir about 5 minutes or until softened. Add to bowl with broccoli. Stir in artichokes.

4 Melt remaining 3 tablespoons butter in same skillet. Stir in flour until blended. Add broth, mustard, salt, tarragon and pepper; cook and stir about 2 minutes or until sauce thickens. Add Emmentaler cheese; stir until smooth. Alternately layer chicken and vegetable mixture in prepared baking dish. Pour cheese sauce over top of casserole.

5 Cover and bake 40 minutes. Uncover; sprinkle with Asiago cheese. Bake 5 to 10 minutes or until cheese is melted.

CHICKEN ZUCCHINI CASSEROLE

MAKES 8 SERVINGS

1 package (about 6 ounces) herb-flavored stuffing mix

½ cup (1 stick) butter, melted

2 cups cubed zucchini

1½ cups chopped cooked chicken

1 can (10¾ ounces) condensed cream of celery soup, undiluted

1 cup grated carrots

1 onion, chopped

½ cup sour cream

½ cup (2 ounces) shredded Cheddar cheese

1 Preheat oven to 350°F.

2 Combine stuffing mix and butter in medium bowl; reserve 1 cup stuffing. Spread remaining stuffing in 13×9-inch baking dish.

3 Combine zucchini, chicken, soup, carrots, onion and sour cream in large bowl; mix well. Pour over stuffing in baking dish; top with reserved 1 cup stuffing and cheese.

4 Bake 40 to 45 minutes or until heated through and cheese is melted.

ARTICHOKE-OLIVE CHICKEN BAKE

MAKES 8 SERVINGS

1½ cups uncooked rotini pasta

1 tablespoon olive oil

1 medium onion, chopped

½ green bell pepper, chopped

2 cups shredded cooked chicken

1 can (about 14 ounces) diced tomatoes with Italian seasoning

1 can (14 ounces) artichoke hearts, drained and quartered

1 can (6 ounces) sliced black olives, drained

1 teaspoon Italian seasoning

2 cups (8 ounces) shredded mozzarella cheese

1 Preheat oven to 350°F. Spray 2-quart casserole with nonstick cooking spray.

2 Cook pasta according to package directions; drain well.

3 Meanwhile, heat oil in large skillet over medium heat. Add onion and bell pepper; cook and stir 1 minute. Add pasta, chicken, tomatoes, artichokes, olives and Italian seasoning; stir gently until blended.

4 Transfer half of chicken mixture to prepared casserole; sprinkle with half of cheese. Top with remaining chicken mixture and cheese.

5 Cover and bake 35 minutes or until hot and bubbly.

TURKEY-TORTILLA CASSEROLE

MAKES 4 SERVINGS

9 (6-inch) corn tortillas

½ pound ground turkey

½ cup chopped onion

¾ cup taco sauce

1 can (4 ounces) chopped mild green chiles, drained

½ cup frozen corn, thawed and drained

½ cup (2 ounces) shredded Cheddar cheese

Sour cream (optional)

1 Preheat oven to 400°F.

2 Place tortillas on large baking sheet, overlapping as little as possible. Bake 4 minutes. Turn tortillas; bake 2 minutes or until crisp. Remove to wire rack to cool completely.

3 Heat medium nonstick skillet over medium heat. Add turkey and onion; cook and stir 5 minutes or until turkey is browned and onion is tender. Stir in taco sauce, chiles and corn; mix well. Reduce heat to low; cook 5 minutes.

4 Break up 3 tortillas; arrange pieces on bottom of 1½-quart casserole. Spoon half of turkey mixture over tortillas; sprinkle with half of cheese. Repeat layers.

5 Bake 10 minutes or until casserole is heated through and cheese is melted. Break remaining 3 tortillas into pieces; sprinkle over casserole. Serve with sour cream, if desired.

COUNTRY CHICKEN POT PIE

MAKES 6 SERVINGS

2 tablespoons butter

1 pound boneless skinless chicken breasts, cut into 1-inch pieces

¾ teaspoon salt

8 ounces fresh green beans, cut into 1-inch pieces (2 cups)

½ cup chopped red bell pepper

½ cup thinly sliced celery

3 tablespoons all-purpose flour

½ cup chicken broth

½ cup half-and-half

1 teaspoon dried thyme

½ teaspoon dried sage

1 cup frozen pearl onions

½ cup frozen corn

Pastry for single-crust 10-inch pie

1 Preheat oven to 425°F. Spray 10-inch deep-dish pie plate with nonstick cooking spray.

2 Melt butter in large skillet over medium-high heat. Add chicken; cook and stir 3 minutes or until no longer pink in center. Sprinkle with salt. Add beans, bell pepper and celery; cook and stir 3 minutes.

3 Sprinkle flour over chicken and vegetables; cook and stir 1 minute. Stir in broth, half-and-half, thyme and sage; bring to a boil over high heat. Reduce heat to low; cook 3 minutes or until sauce is thickened. Stir in onions and corn. Return to a simmer; cook and stir 1 minute.

4 Transfer mixture to prepared pie plate. Place pie crust over filling; turn edge under and flute or crimp. Cut four slits in top of crust with tip of knife.

5 Bake 20 minutes or until filling is hot and bubbly and crust is golden brown. Let stand 5 minutes before serving.

SEAFOOD

BAKED HALIBUT CREOLE

MAKES 4 SERVINGS

4 fresh or thawed frozen (1-inch thick) halibut steaks (about 1½ pounds total)

Salt and black pepper

1 can (8 ounces) tomato sauce

1 package (12 ounces) frozen mixed vegetables such as broccoli, peas, onions and bell peppers

Hot cooked rice (optional)

1 Preheat oven to 350°F.

2 Rinse halibut; place in 13×9-inch baking pan. Season with salt and pepper.

3 Top fish with tomato sauce and mixed vegetables; season with additional salt and pepper.

4 Bake 25 to 30 minutes or until fish begins to flake when tested with fork. Serve over rice, if desired.

CREAMY SHRIMP AND VEGETABLE CASSEROLE

MAKES 4 SERVINGS

- 1 pound fresh or thawed frozen medium raw shrimp, peeled and deveined
- 1 can (10¾ ounces) condensed cream of celery soup, undiluted
- ½ cup sliced fresh or thawed frozen asparagus (1-inch pieces)
- ½ cup sliced mushrooms
- ¼ cup diced red bell pepper
- ¼ cup sliced green onions
- 1 clove garlic, minced
- ¾ teaspoon dried thyme
- ¼ teaspoon black pepper
- Hot cooked rice or orzo (optional)

1 Preheat oven to 375°F. Spray 2-quart baking dish with nonstick cooking spray.

2 Combine shrimp, soup, asparagus, mushrooms, bell pepper, green onions, garlic, thyme and black pepper in large bowl; mix well. Transfer to prepared baking dish.

3 Cover and bake 30 minutes. Serve over rice, if desired.

SEAFOOD PASTA

MAKES 6 SERVINGS

¼ cup olive oil

1 pound asparagus, trimmed and cut into 1-inch pieces

1 cup chopped green onions

1 tablespoon minced garlic

1 package (16 ounces) linguine, cooked and drained

1 pound medium cooked shrimp, peeled and deveined

1 package (8 ounces) imitation crabmeat

1 package (8 ounces) imitation lobster

1 can (8 ounces) pitted black olives, drained

1 Preheat oven to 350°F. Spray 4-quart casserole with nonstick cooking spray.

2 Heat oil in large skillet over medium heat. Add asparagus, green onions and garlic; cook and stir 5 minutes.

3 Combine asparagus mixture, linguine, shrimp, crabmeat, lobster and olives in prepared casserole; stir gently.

4 Bake 30 minutes or until heated through.

TUNA TOMATO CASSEROLE

MAKES 6 SERVINGS

2 cans (6 ounces each) tuna, drained and flaked

1 cup mayonnaise

1 onion, finely chopped

½ teaspoon salt

¼ teaspoon black pepper

1 package (12 ounces) wide egg noodles, uncooked

8 to 10 plum tomatoes, sliced ¼ inch thick

1 cup (4 ounces) shredded Cheddar or mozzarella cheese

1 Preheat oven to 375°F.

2 Combine tuna, mayonnaise, onion, salt and pepper in medium bowl; mix well.

3 Cook noodles according to package directions; drain and return to saucepan. Gently stir in tuna mixture until well blended.

4 Layer half of noodle mixture, half of tomatoes and half of cheese in 13×9-inch baking dish; press down slightly. Repeat layers.

5 Bake 20 minutes or until casserole is heated through and cheese is melted.

SHRIMP CREOLE

MAKES 4 TO 6 SERVINGS

2 tablespoons olive oil

1½ cups chopped green
  bell peppers

1 medium onion,
  chopped

⅔ cup chopped celery

2 cloves garlic, minced

1 cup uncooked rice

1 can (about 14 ounces)
  diced tomatoes,
  drained and liquid
  reserved

2 teaspoons hot pepper
  sauce, or to taste

1 teaspoon dried
  oregano

¾ teaspoon salt

½ teaspoon dried thyme

  Black pepper

1 pound medium raw
  shrimp, peeled
  and deveined
  (with tails on)

  Chopped fresh parsley
  (optional)

1 Preheat oven to 325°F.

2 Heat oil in large skillet over medium-high heat.
  Add bell peppers, onion, celery and garlic;
  cook and stir 5 minutes or until vegetables
  are tender.

3 Add rice; cook and stir over medium heat
  5 minutes. Add tomatoes, hot pepper sauce,
  oregano, salt, thyme and black pepper; stir
  until well blended.

4 Pour reserved tomato liquid into measuring
  cup; add enough water to measure 1¾ cups.
  Add to skillet; cook and stir 2 minutes. Stir
  in shrimp. Transfer to 2½-quart casserole.

5 Cover and bake 55 minutes or until rice is
  tender and liquid is absorbed. Garnish
  with parsley.

SCALLOP AND ARTICHOKE CASSEROLE

MAKES 4 SERVINGS

1 package (9 ounces) frozen artichoke hearts, cooked and drained

1 pound scallops

1 tablespoon canola or vegetable oil

¼ cup chopped red bell pepper

¼ cup sliced green onions

¼ cup all-purpose flour

2 cups milk

1 teaspoon dried tarragon

¼ teaspoon salt

¼ teaspoon white pepper

1 tablespoon chopped fresh parsley

Dash paprika

1 Preheat oven to 350°F.

2 Cut large artichoke hearts lengthwise into halves. Arrange artichokes in even layer in 8-inch square baking dish.

3 Rinse scallops; pat dry with paper towel. If scallops are large, cut into halves. Arrange scallops evenly over artichokes.

4 Heat oil in medium saucepan over medium-low heat. Add bell pepper and green onions; cook and stir 5 minutes or until tender. Stir in flour until blended. Gradually stir in milk until smooth. Add tarragon, salt and white pepper; cook and stir over medium heat 10 minutes or until sauce boils and thickens. Pour sauce over scallops.

5 Bake 25 minutes or until casserole is bubbly and scallops are opaque. Sprinkle with parsley and paprika.

TUNA PENNE CASSEROLE

6 ounces penne pasta, uncooked

1 can (10¾ ounces) condensed cream of chicken soup, undiluted

1 can (about 6 ounces) tuna, drained and flaked

1 cup (4 ounces) shredded sharp Cheddar cheese

½ cup sliced celery

½ cup milk

¼ cup mayonnaise

1 can (4 ounces) sliced water chestnuts, drained

1 jar (2 ounces) chopped pimientos, drained

½ teaspoon salt

Dash black pepper

Pinch celery seed

1 Preheat oven to 350°F. Spray 2-quart casserole with nonstick cooking spray.

2 Cook pasta according to package directions; drain and return to saucepan.

3 Add soup, tuna, cheese celery, milk, mayonnaise, water chestnuts, pimientos, salt, pepper and celery seed; mix well. Transfer to prepared casserole.

4 Bake 25 minutes or until hot and bubbly.

SEAFOOD GRATIN

MAKES 6 SERVINGS

8 ounces cooked shrimp

8 ounces cooked
   crabmeat

8 ounces cooked sole

8 ounces cooked lobster

2 tablespoons butter

2 tablespoons
   all-purpose flour

½ cup milk

¾ cup grated Parmesan
   cheese

½ cup cola

Bread crumbs or
   panko

1 Preheat oven to 325°F. Spray six individual gratin dishes or 2-quart baking dish with nonstick cooking spray.

2 Cut seafood into bite-sized pieces; place in prepared dishes.

3 Melt butter in small saucepan over medium heat. Add flour; stir until blended. Cook until mixture is lightly browned; stirring constantly. Stir in milk and cheese until smooth. When mixture is slightly thickened, stir in cola.

4 Pour sauce over seafood; sprinkle with bread crumbs.

5 Bake 20 minutes or until bubbly and golden brown. Let stand 5 minutes before serving.

CRUSTLESS SALMON AND BROCCOLI QUICHE

MAKES 4 SERVINGS

- 3 eggs
- ¼ cup chopped green onions
- ¼ cup plain yogurt
- 2 teaspoons all-purpose flour
- 1 teaspoon dried basil
- ½ teaspoon salt
- ⅛ teaspoon black pepper
- ¾ cup frozen broccoli florets, thawed and drained
- 1 can (6 ounces) boneless skinless salmon, drained and flaked
- 2 tablespoons grated Parmesan cheese
- 1 plum tomato, thinly sliced
- ¼ cup fresh bread crumbs

1 Preheat oven to 375°F. Spray 1½-quart casserole or 9-inch deep-dish pie plate with nonstick cooking spray.

2 Whisk eggs, green onions, yogurt, flour, basil, salt and pepper in medium bowl until well blended. Stir in broccoli, salmon and cheese.

3 Transfer mixture to prepared casserole. Top with tomato slices; sprinkle with bread crumbs.

4 Bake 20 to 25 minutes or until knife inserted near center comes out clean. Let stand 5 minutes before serving.

SEAFOOD NEWBURG CASSEROLE

MAKES 6 SERVINGS

1 can (10¾ ounces) condensed cream of shrimp soup, undiluted

½ cup half-and-half

1 tablespoon dry sherry

¼ teaspoon ground red pepper

2 cans (6 ounces each) lump crabmeat, drained

3 cups cooked rice

4 ounces medium raw shrimp, peeled and deveined

4 ounces bay scallops, rinsed and patted dry

1 jar (4 ounces) pimientos, drained and chopped

2 tablespoons finely chopped fresh parsley

1 Preheat oven to 350°F. Spray 2½-quart casserole with nonstick cooking spray.

2 Combine soup, half-and-half, sherry and red pepper in large bowl; mix well.

3 Pick out and discard any shell or cartilage from crabmeat. Add crabmeat, rice, shrimp, scallops and pimientos to soup mixture; mix well. Transfer to prepared casserole.

4 Cover and bake 25 minutes or until shrimp and scallops are opaque. Sprinkle with parsley.

SHRIMP AND CHICKEN PAELLA

MAKES 4 SERVINGS

¾ cup cooked rice

2 cans (about 14 ounces each) diced tomatoes

½ teaspoon ground turmeric *or* ⅛ teaspoon saffron threads

1 package (12 ounces) medium raw shrimp, peeled and deveined (with tails on)

2 chicken tenders (about 4 ounces), cut into 1-inch pieces

1 cup frozen peas

1 Preheat oven to 400°F. Spray 8-inch square baking dish with nonstick cooking spray.

2 Spread rice in prepared baking dish. Pour 1 can of tomatoes over rice; sprinkle with turmeric. Arrange shrimp and chicken over tomatoes; top with peas.

3 Drain remaining can of tomatoes, discarding juice. Spread tomatoes evenly over shrimp and chicken.

4 Cover and bake 30 minutes. Let stand, covered, 5 minutes before serving.

EASY CRAB-ASPARAGUS PIE

MAKES 6 SERVINGS

4 ounces crabmeat (fresh, frozen or pasteurized)

1½ cups sliced asparagus, cooked

½ cup chopped onion, cooked

1 cup (4 ounces) shredded Monterey Jack cheese

¼ cup grated Parmesan cheese

Black pepper

¾ cup all-purpose flour

¾ teaspoon baking powder

½ teaspoon salt

2 tablespoons butter

1½ cups milk

4 eggs, lightly beaten

1 Preheat oven to 350°F. Spray 10-inch quiche dish or deep-dish pie plate.

2 Pick out and discard any shell or cartilage from crabmeat. Layer crabmeat, asparagus and onion in prepared quiche dish; top with cheeses. Season with pepper.

3 Combine flour, baking powder and salt in large bowl. Cut in butter with pastry blender or two knives until mixture forms coarse crumbs. Stir in milk and eggs until blended. Pour over crabmeat mixture and cheeses.

4 Bake 30 minutes or until puffed and knife inserted near center comes out clean.

SALMON NOODLE CASSEROLE

MAKES 4 SERVINGS

6 ounces uncooked wide egg noodles

1 tablespoon vegetable oil

1 onion, finely chopped

¾ cup thinly sliced carrot

¾ cup thinly sliced celery

1 can (about 15 ounces) salmon, drained, skin and bones discarded

1 can (10¾ ounces) condensed cream of celery soup, undiluted

1 cup (4 ounces) shredded Cheddar cheese

¾ cup frozen peas

½ cup sour cream

¼ cup milk

2 teaspoons dried dill weed

Black pepper

Chopped fresh dill (optional)

1 Preheat oven to 350°F.

2 Cook noodles according to package directions; drain and return to saucepan.

3 Heat oil in large skillet over medium heat. Add onion, carrot and celery; cook and stir 5 minutes or until carrot is crisp-tender. Add to noodles with salmon, soup, cheese, peas, sour cream, milk, dill weed and pepper; stir gently to coat. Transfer to 2-quart baking dish.

4 Cover and bake 25 minutes or until hot and bubbly. Garnish with fresh dill.

VEGETABLES & SIDES

SWEET POTATO AND APPLE CASSEROLE

MAKES 9 SERVINGS

1 cup all-purpose flour

¾ cup (1½ sticks) butter, melted, divided

½ cup packed brown sugar

½ teaspoon salt

½ teaspoon ground cinnamon

¼ teaspoon ground nutmeg or mace

¼ teaspoon ground cardamom

2 pounds sweet potatoes, peeled, halved lengthwise and thinly sliced

2 Granny Smith apples, peeled, halved lengthwise and thinly sliced

1 Preheat oven to 375°F. Spray 2-quart baking dish with nonstick cooking spray.

2 Combine flour, ½ cup butter, brown sugar, salt, cinnamon, nutmeg and cardamom in medium bowl until well blended.

3 Arrange sweet potatoes and apples in prepared baking dish. Drizzle with remaining ¼ cup butter; season lightly with salt. Crumble topping over sweet potatoes and apples.

4 Bake 35 to 40 minutes or until topping is browned and potatoes and apples are tender.

SOUTHWEST SPAGHETTI SQUASH

MAKES 4 SERVINGS

1 spaghetti squash
  (about 3 pounds)

1 can (about 14 ounces)
  Mexican-style diced
  tomatoes

1 can (about 14 ounces)
  black beans, rinsed
  and drained

¾ cup (3 ounces)
  shredded Monterey
  Jack cheese, divided

¼ cup finely chopped
  fresh cilantro

1 teaspoon ground
  cumin

¼ teaspoon garlic salt

¼ teaspoon black
  pepper

1 Preheat oven to 350°F. Spray baking sheet
  and 1½-quart baking dish with nonstick
  cooking spray.

2 Cut squash in half lengthwise; remove and
  discard seeds. Place squash, cut side down,
  on prepared baking sheet.

3 Bake 45 minutes or just until tender. Shred
  squash with fork; place in large bowl. (Use
  oven mitts to protect hands.)

4 Add tomatoes, beans, ½ cup cheese, cilantro,
  cumin, garlic salt and pepper; mix well.
  Transfer to prepared baking dish; sprinkle
  with remaining ¼ cup cheese.

5 Bake 30 to 35 minutes or until heated through.

SPIRALED VEGETABLE ENCHILADAS

MAKES 6 SERVINGS

1 large zucchini

1 large red onion

2 large poblano peppers or green bell peppers

1 tablespoon vegetable oil

1 cup sliced mushrooms

1 teaspoon ground cumin

1 pound fresh tomatillos (about 8 large), peeled

½ to 1 jalapeño pepper, minced*

1 clove garlic

½ teaspoon salt

1 cup loosely packed fresh cilantro, plus additional for garnish

12 corn tortillas, warmed

2 cups (8 ounces) shredded Mexican cheese blend, divided

Jalapeño peppers can sting and irritate the skin, so wear rubber gloves when handling peppers and do not touch your eyes.

1 Preheat oven to 400°F.

2 Spiral zucchini and red onion with thick spiral blade. Spiral poblano peppers with spiral slicing blade.* Cut vegetables into desired lengths.

3 Heat oil in large nonstick skillet over medium heat. Add poblano peppers, zucchini, onion, mushrooms and cumin; cook and stir 8 to 10 minutes or until vegetables are crisp-tender.

4 Meanwhile, place tomatillos in large microwavable bowl; cover with vented plastic wrap. Microwave on HIGH 6 to 7 minutes or until very tender.

5 Combine tomatillos with juice, jalapeño, garlic and salt in food processor or blender; process until smooth. Add 1 cup cilantro; pulse until combined and cilantro is coarsely chopped.

6 Divide vegetables evenly among tortillas. Spoon heaping tablespoon of cheese in center of each tortilla; roll up to enclose filling. Place in 13×9-inch baking dish. Pour sauce evenly over enchiladas; sprinkle with remaining 1 cup cheese.

7 Cover and bake 18 to 20 minutes or until cheese is melted and enchiladas are heated through. Garnish with additional cilantro. Serve immediately.

If you don't have a spiralizer, cut vegetables into thin strips.

SPINACH ARTICHOKE GRATIN

MAKES 6 SERVINGS

2 cups (16 ounces) cottage cheese

2 eggs

4½ tablespoons grated Parmesan cheese, divided

1 tablespoon lemon juice

¼ teaspoon salt

⅛ teaspoon black pepper

⅛ teaspoon ground nutmeg

2 packages (10 ounces each) frozen chopped spinach, thawed

⅓ cup thinly sliced green onions

1 package (10 ounces) frozen artichoke hearts, thawed and halved

1. Preheat oven to 375°F. Spray 1½-quart baking dish with nonstick cooking spray.

2. Combine cottage cheese, eggs, 3 tablespoons Parmesan, lemon juice, salt, pepper and nutmeg in food processor or blender; process until smooth.

3. Squeeze moisture from spinach. Combine spinach, cottage cheese mixture and green onions in large bowl; mix well. Spread half of mixture in prepared baking dish.

4. Pat artichokes dry with paper towels; arrange in single layer over spinach mixture. Sprinkle with remaining 1½ tablespoons Parmesan; top with remaining spinach mixture.

5. Cover and bake 25 minutes.

FRUITED CORN PUDDING

MAKES 8 SERVINGS

5 cups thawed frozen corn, divided

5 eggs

½ cup milk

1½ cups whipping cream

⅓ cup unsalted butter, melted and cooled

1 teaspoon vanilla

½ teaspoon salt

¼ teaspoon ground nutmeg

3 tablespoons finely chopped dried apricots

3 tablespoons dried cranberries or raisins

3 tablespoons finely chopped dates

2 tablespoons finely chopped dried pears or other dried fruit

1 Preheat oven to 350°F. Spray 13×9-inch baking dish with nonstick cooking spray.

2 Combine 3½ cups corn, eggs and milk in food processor; process until almost smooth.

3 Transfer to large bowl. Add cream, butter, vanilla, salt and nutmeg; stir until well blended. Add remaining 1½ cups corn, apricots, cranberries, dates and pears; mix well. Pour into prepared baking dish.

4 Bake 50 to 60 minutes or until center is set and top begins to brown. Let stand 10 to 15 minutes before serving.

ZUCCHINI WITH FETA CASSEROLE

MAKES 4 SERVINGS

4 medium zucchini

1 tablespoon butter

2 eggs, beaten

½ cup grated Parmesan cheese

⅓ cup crumbled feta cheese

2 tablespoons chopped fresh parsley

1 tablespoon all-purpose flour

2 teaspoons chopped fresh marjoram

Dash hot pepper sauce

Salt and black pepper

1 Preheat oven to 375°F. Spray 2-quart casserole with nonstick cooking spray.

2 Grate zucchini; drain in colander. Melt butter in large skillet over medium heat. Add zucchini; cook and stir until slightly browned.

3 Remove from heat; stir in eggs, cheeses, parsley, flour, marjoram, hot pepper sauce, salt and black pepper until well blended. Transfer to prepared casserole.

4 Bake 35 minutes or until hot and bubbly.

MEXICAN RICE OLÉ

MAKES 4 SERVINGS

1 teaspoon vegetable oil

1 cup uncooked long grain rice

1 teaspoon salt

1 clove garlic, minced

1 can (about 14 ounces) chicken broth

1 can (10¾ ounces) condensed cream of chicken soup, undiluted

¾ cup sour cream

1 can (4 ounces) chopped mild green chiies, undrained

⅓ cup salsa

1 teaspoon ground cumin

1 cup (4 ounces) shredded Cheddar cheese

1 can (about 2 ounces) sliced black olives, drained

1 Preheat oven to 350°F. Spray 3-quart casserole with nonstick cooking spray.

2 Heat oil in large skillet over medium heat. Add rice, salt and garlic; cook and stir 2 to 3 minutes or until rice is well coated.

3 Add enough water to broth to equal 2 cups. Pour into skillet; cook about 15 minutes or until rice is tender, stirring occasionally.

4 Remove from heat; stir in soup, sour cream, chiles, salsa and cumin until blended. Transfer to prepared casserole.

5 Bake 20 minutes. Sprinkle with cheese and olives; bake 5 to 10 minutes or until cheese is melted and casserole is heated through.

WILD RICE MUSHROOM STUFFING

MAKES 6 TO 8 SERVINGS

½ cup uncooked wild rice

Day-old French bread (about 4 ounces)

½ cup (1 stick) butter

1 large onion, chopped

1 clove garlic, minced

3 cups sliced mushrooms

½ teaspoon rubbed sage

½ teaspoon dried thyme

½ teaspoon salt

¼ teaspoon black pepper

1 cup chicken broth

½ cup coarsely chopped pecans

Fresh thyme sprigs (optional)

1 Prepare rice according to package directions. Preheat broiler.

2 Cut enough bread into ½-inch cubes to measure 4 cups. Spread in single layer on baking sheet. Broil 5 to 6 inches from heat 4 minutes or until lightly toasted, stirring after 2 minutes. *Reduce oven temperature to 325°F.*

3 Melt butter in large skillet over medium heat. Add onion and garlic; cook and stir 3 minutes. Add mushrooms; cook 5 minutes, stirring occasionally. Add sage, dried thyme, salt, pepper and cooked rice; cook 2 minutes, stirring occasionally. Stir in broth. Add pecans and toasted bread cubes; toss gently. Transfer to 1½-quart casserole.

4 Cover and bake 40 minutes or until heated through. Garnish with fresh thyme.

CHILES RELLENOS CASSEROLE

MAKES 4 SERVINGS

 3 eggs, separated

¾ cup milk

¾ cup all-purpose flour

½ teaspoon salt

 1 tablespoon butter

½ cup chopped onion

 2 cans (7 ounces each) whole green chiles, drained

 8 slices (1 ounce each) Monterey Jack cheese, cut into halves

 Toppings: sour cream, sliced green onions, sliced olives, guacamole and salsa

1 Preheat oven to 350°F. Spray 13×9-inch baking dish with nonstick cooking spray.

2 Combine egg yolks, milk, flour and salt in food processor or blender; process until smooth. Pour into large bowl.

3 Melt butter in small skillet over medium heat. Add onion; cook and stir until tender.

4 Pat chiles dry with paper towels. Slit each chile lengthwise and remove seeds. Place 2 halves of cheese and 1 tablespoon onion inside each chile; reshape chiles to cover cheese. Place in single layer in prepared baking dish.

5 Beat egg whites in medium bowl with electric mixer at medium-high speed until soft peaks form; fold into yolk mixture. Pour over chiles in baking dish.

6 Bake 20 to 25 minutes or until casserole is puffed and knife inserted into center comes out clean. Broil 4 inches from heat source 30 seconds or until top is golden brown. Serve with desired toppings.

GREEK SPINACH AND FETA PIE

MAKES 6 SERVINGS

⅓ cup butter, melted

2 eggs

1 container (15 ounces) ricotta cheese

1 package (10 ounces) frozen chopped spinach, thawed and squeezed dry

1 package (4 ounces) crumbled feta cheese

¾ teaspoon finely grated lemon peel

¼ teaspoon black pepper

⅛ teaspoon ground nutmeg

1 package (16 ounces) frozen phyllo dough, thawed

1 Preheat oven to 350°F. Brush 13×9-inch baking dish lightly with some of butter.

2 Beat eggs in medium bowl. Stir in ricotta, spinach, feta, lemon peel, pepper and nutmeg until well blended.

3 Unwrap phyllo dough; remove 8 sheets. Cut phyllo in half crosswise to form 16 rectangles about 13×8½ inches each. Cover phyllo with damp cloth or plastic wrap to prevent drying out. Reserve remaining phyllo for another use.

4 Place 1 piece of phyllo in prepared baking dish; brush top lightly with butter. Layer with another piece of phyllo and brush lightly with butter. Continue layering with 6 pieces of phyllo, brushing each lightly with butter. Spread spinach mixture evenly over phyllo.

5 Top spinach mixture with 1 piece of phyllo; brush lightly with butter. Repeat layering with remaining 7 pieces of phyllo, brushing each piece lightly with butter.

6 Bake 35 to 40 minutes or until golden brown.

POTATO AND LEEK GRATIN

MAKES 6 TO 8 SERVINGS

5 tablespoons butter, divided

2 large leeks, sliced

2 tablespoons minced garlic

2 pounds baking potatoes, peeled (about 4 medium)

1 cup whipping cream

1 cup milk

3 eggs

2 teaspoons salt

¼ teaspoon white pepper

2 to 3 slices dense day-old white bread, such as French or Italian

2 ounces grated Parmesan cheese

1 Preheat oven to 375°F. Generously grease shallow 2½-quart baking dish with 1 tablespoon butter.

2 Melt 2 tablespoons butter in large skillet over medium heat. Add leeks and garlic; cook and stir 8 to 10 minutes or until leeks are softened. Remove from heat.

3 Cut potatoes crosswise into ¹⁄₁₆-inch-thick slices. Layer half of potato slices in prepared baking dish; top with half of leek mixture. Repeat layers. Whisk cream, milk, eggs, salt and pepper in medium bowl until well blended; pour evenly over leek mixture.

4 Tear bread slices into 1-inch pieces. Place in food processor; process until fine crumbs form. Measure ¾ cup crumbs; place in small bowl. Stir in Parmesan. Melt remaining 2 tablespoons butter; stir into crumb mixture. Sprinkle over vegetables in baking dish.

5 Bake about 1 hour 15 minutes or until top is golden brown and potatoes are tender. Let stand 5 to 10 minutes before serving.

POLENTA LASAGNA

MAKES 6 SERVINGS

4¼ cups water, divided

1½ cups yellow cornmeal

4 teaspoons finely chopped fresh marjoram

2 medium red bell peppers, chopped

1 tablespoon olive oil

1 pound fresh mushrooms, sliced

1 cup chopped leeks

1 clove garlic, minced

½ cup (2 ounces) shredded mozzarella cheese

2 tablespoons chopped fresh basil

1 tablespoon chopped fresh oregano

⅛ teaspoon black pepper

4 tablespoons grated Parmesan cheese

1 Bring 4 cups water to a boil in medium saucepan over high heat. Slowly add cornmeal, stirring constantly. Reduce heat to low; stir in marjoram. Cook 15 to 20 minutes or until polenta thickens and pulls away from side of pan. Spread in ungreased 13×9-inch baking pan. Cover and refrigerate about 1 hour or until firm.

2 Preheat oven to 350°F. Spray 11×7-inch baking dish with nonstick cooking spray. Combine bell peppers and remaining ¼ cup water in food processor or blender; process until smooth.

3 Heat oil in large nonstick skillet over medium heat. Add mushrooms, leeks and garlic; cook and stir 5 minutes or until leeks are crisp-tender. Stir in mozzarella, basil, oregano and black pepper.

4 Cut cold polenta into 12 (3½-inch) squares; arrange six squares in prepared baking dish. Top with half of bell pepper mixture, half of vegetable mixture and 2 tablespoons Parmesan. Repeat layers.

5 Bake 20 minutes or until polenta is golden brown and cheese is melted.

MEDITERRANEAN VEGETABLE BAKE

MAKES 4 TO 6 SERVINGS

2 tomatoes, sliced

1 small red onion, sliced

1 medium zucchini, sliced

1 small eggplant, sliced

1 small yellow squash, sliced

1 large portobello mushroom, sliced

2 cloves garlic, finely chopped

3 tablespoons olive oil

2 teaspoons fresh rosemary leaves

⅔ cup dry white wine

Salt and black pepper

1 Preheat oven to 350°F. Spray bottom of oval casserole or 13×9-inch baking dish with nonstick cooking spray.

2 Arrange slices of vegetables in rows, alternating different types and overlapping slices; sprinkle with garlic. Combine oil and rosemary in small bowl; drizzle over vegetables.

3 Pour wine over vegetables; season with salt and pepper. Cover loosely with foil.

4 Bake 20 minutes. Uncover; bake 10 to 15 minutes or until vegetables are tender.

PASTA & NOODLES

BOWTIE ZUCCHINI

MAKES 8 SERVINGS

¼ cup vegetable oil

1 cup chopped onion

2 cloves garlic, minced

5 small zucchini, cut into thin strips

⅔ cup whipping cream

1 package (16 ounces) bowtie pasta, cooked and drained

3 tablespoons grated Parmesan cheese

Salt and black pepper

1 Preheat oven to 350°F.

2 Heat oil in large skillet over medium-high heat. Add onion and garlic; cook and stir 3 minutes or until onion is translucent. Add zucchini; cook and stir until tender.

3 Add cream; cook and stir until thickened. Add pasta and cheese to skillet; season with salt and pepper. Transfer to 2-quart casserole.

4 Cover and bake 15 minutes or until heated through.

BAKED PASTA CASSEROLE

MAKES 2 SERVINGS

1½ cups (3 ounces) uncooked wagon wheel (rotelle) pasta

4 ounces ground beef

2 tablespoons chopped onion

2 tablespoons chopped green bell pepper

1 clove garlic, minced

½ cup pasta sauce

Dash black pepper

2 tablespoons shredded Italian-style mozzarella and Parmesan cheese blend

1 Preheat oven to 350°F. Cook pasta according to package directions; drain and return to saucepan.

2 Meanwhile, combine beef, onion, bell pepper and garlic in large nonstick skillet; cook and stir over medium-high heat 3 to 4 minutes or until beef is no longer pink and vegetables are crisp-tender. Drain fat.

3 Add beef mixture, pasta sauce and black pepper to pasta in saucepan; mix well. Transfer to 1-quart baking dish; sprinkle with cheese.

4 Bake 15 minutes or until heated through.

TIP: To make ahead, assemble casserole as directed above through step 3. Cover and refrigerate several hours or overnight. Bake, uncovered, in preheated 350°F oven 30 minutes or until heated through.

RAMEN REUBEN NOODLE BAKE

MAKES 8 SERVINGS

6 cups water

3 packages (3 ounces each) beef-flavored ramen noodles

¼ cup (½ stick) butter, melted

2 cans (14 ounces each) shredded sauerkraut, undrained

1 pound deli corned beef, thinly sliced and chopped

1½ teaspoons caraway seeds, divided

½ cup Thousand Island dressing

8 slices (6 ounces) Swiss cheese

1 Preheat oven to 350°F. Spray 13×9-inch baking dish with nonstick cooking spray.

2 Bring water to a boil in large saucepan over high heat. Add noodles and seasoning packets; return to a boil. Cook 2 to 3 minutes or until al dente; drain well.

3 Combine noodles, butter, sauerkraut with liquid, corned beef and 1 teaspoon caraway seeds in large bowl; toss to coat. Transfer to prepared baking dish.

4 Cover and bake 20 minutes or until heated through. Drizzle with dressing; top with cheese and remaining ½ teaspoon caraway seeds. Bake, uncovered, 13 to 15 minutes or until casserole is bubbly and cheese is melted.

TOMATO, BRIE & NOODLE CASSEROLE

MAKES 6 SERVINGS

1 pint grape tomatoes, halved

2 teaspoons olive oil

¾ teaspoon salt, divided

2 tablespoons butter

1 clove garlic, smashed

2 tablespoons all-purpose flour

2 cups half-and-half, heated

8 ounces good-quality ripe Brie, crust removed, cut into small chunks

¼ cup finely chopped fresh basil

2 tablespoons minced fresh chives

¼ teaspoon black pepper

6 ounces egg noodles, cooked (about 3½ to 4 cups uncooked)

¼ cup sliced almonds

1 Preheat oven to 425°F. Line baking sheet with heavy-duty foil. Spray 9-inch square baking dish with nonstick cooking spray.

2 Spread tomatoes on baking sheet; sprinkle with oil and ¼ teaspoon salt. Roast 20 minutes or until tomatoes are tender and slightly shriveled. Set aside. *Reduce oven temperature to 350°F.*

3 Melt butter in large saucepan or deep skillet over medium heat. Add garlic; cook and stir 1 minute. Stir in flour until blended. Gradually add half-and-half; cook and stir until thickened. Remove and discard garlic. Gradually stir in cheese until melted.

4 Add basil, chives, remaining ½ teaspoon salt and pepper. Stir in noodles. Drain off any liquid from tomatoes; fold into noodle mixture. Transfer to prepared baking dish.

5 Bake 17 to 20 minutes or until sauce begins to bubble. Sprinkle with almonds; bake 8 to 10 minutes or until nuts are golden brown.

MUSHROOM GRATIN

MAKES 8 SERVINGS

4 tablespoons butter, divided

1 small onion, minced

8 ounces (about 2½ cups) sliced cremini mushrooms

2 cloves garlic, minced

4 cups cooked elbow macaroni, rotini or other pasta

2 tablespoons all-purpose flour

1 cup milk

½ teaspoon salt

½ teaspoon black pepper

½ teaspoon dry mustard

½ cup fresh bread crumbs

1 tablespoon extra virgin olive oil

1 Preheat oven to 350°F. Spray shallow baking dish with nonstick cooking spray.

2 Melt 2 tablespoons butter in large skillet over medium-high heat. Add onion; cook and stir 2 minutes. Add mushrooms and garlic; cook and stir 6 to 8 minutes or until vegetables are softened. Remove from heat; stir in macaroni.

3 Melt remaining 2 tablespoons butter in medium saucepan over low heat. Stir in flour until blended; cook and stir 2 minutes without browning. Gradually add milk; bring to a boil over medium-high heat, stirring constantly. Reduce heat to maintain a simmer. Add salt, pepper and mustard; cook and stir 5 to 7 minutes or until sauce thickens.

4 Pour sauce over mushroom mixture in skillet; stir gently to coat. Transfer to prepared baking dish. Top with bread crumbs; drizzle with oil.

5 Cover and bake 15 minutes. Uncover; bake 10 minutes or until casserole is bubbly and topping is browned.

BAKED VEGETABLE PENNE

MAKES 6 SERVINGS

- 6 ounces (about 2 cups) uncooked whole wheat penne or ziti pasta
- 1 large zucchini
- 1 yellow squash
- 1 red onion
- 1 red bell pepper
- 1 tablespoon olive oil
- 2 cups sliced mushrooms
- 1 teaspoon salt
- 1 teaspoon Italian seasoning
- ½ cup ricotta cheese
- 2 cups pasta sauce, divided
- ½ cup (2 ounces) shredded mozzarella cheese
- 2 tablespoons shredded Parmesan cheese (optional)

1 Preheat oven to 400°F. Spray 11×7-inch baking dish with nonstick cooking spray.

2 Cook pasta according to package directions; drain and return to saucepan.

3 Spiral zucchini, yellow squash and red onion with fine spiral blade. Spiral bell pepper with spiral slice blade. Cut vegetables into desired lengths.*

4 Heat oil in large nonstick skillet over medium-high heat. Add mushrooms; cook and stir 4 minutes or until browned. Add zucchini, yellow squash, onion, bell pepper, salt and Italian seasoning; mix well. Remove from heat.

5 Add ricotta and 1½ cups pasta sauce to pasta; mix gently. Spread half of mixture in prepared baking dish. Top with vegetable mixture, remaining pasta mixture, pasta sauce and mozzarella.

6 Bake 20 minutes or until cheese is melted and begins to brown. Let stand 15 minutes before serving. Sprinkle with Parmesan, if desired.

*If you don't have a spiralizer, cut vegetables into thin strips.

SHELLS AND FONTINA

MAKES 4 TO 6 SERVINGS

8 ounces uncooked small whole wheat pasta shells

1¾ cups milk

4 large fresh sage leaves (optional)

3 tablespoons butter

4 tablespoons all-purpose flour

½ cup tomato sauce

Salt and black pepper

¾ cup grated Parmesan cheese, divided

5½ ounces fontina cheese, shredded*

¼ cup dry bread crumbs

It is easier to shred fontina cheese if it is very cold. Keep it in the refrigerator or place it in the freezer for 10 minutes before shredding.

1 Preheat oven to 350°F.

2 Cook pasta according to package directions until barely al dente. Run under cold running water to stop cooking; drain well.

3 Meanwhile, heat milk with sage leaves, if desired, in small saucepan over medium heat (do not boil). Melt butter in large saucepan over medium-low heat until bubbly. Whisk in flour until blended; cook and stir 2 minutes without browning. Remove sage and gradually whisk in milk over medium heat; cook 4 to 5 minutes or until mixture begins to bubble and thickens slightly, whisking constantly. Stir in tomato sauce; season with salt and pepper. Remove from heat; stir in ½ cup Parmesan until smooth.

4 Add pasta to sauce; stir gently to coat. Spread one third of pasta mixture in 2-quart casserole; top with one third of fontina cheese. Repeat layers twice. Sprinkle with bread crumbs and remaining ¼ cup Parmesan.

5 Bake 20 to 25 minutes or until hot and bubbly.

SPINACH-CHEESE PASTA CASSEROLE

MAKES 6 TO 8 SERVINGS

8 ounces uncooked shell pasta

2 eggs

1 cup ricotta cheese

1 package (10 ounces) frozen chopped spinach, thawed and squeezed dry

1 jar (26 ounces) marinara sauce

1 teaspoon salt

1 cup (4 ounces) shredded mozzarella cheese

¼ cup grated Parmesan cheese

1 Preheat oven to 350°F. Spray 1½-quart casserole with nonstick cooking spray.

2 Cook pasta according to package directions; drain well.

3 Whisk eggs in large bowl until blended. Add ricotta and spinach; stir until blended. Stir in pasta, marinara sauce and salt until pasta is well coated. Pour into prepared casserole; sprinkle with cheeses.

4 Cover and bake 30 minutes. Uncover; bake 15 minutes or until hot and bubbly.

PUMPKIN MAC AND CHEESE

MAKES 6 TO 8 SERVINGS

1 package (16 ounces) uncooked large elbow macaroni

½ cup (1 stick) butter, divided

¼ cup all-purpose flour

1½ cups milk

1 teaspoon salt, divided

¼ teaspoon ground nutmeg

⅛ teaspoon ground red pepper

2 cups (8 ounces) shredded Cheddar cheese

1 cup (4 ounces) shredded Monterey Jack cheese

1 cup canned pumpkin

1 cup panko bread crumbs

½ cup chopped hazelnuts or walnuts (optional)

⅛ teaspoon dried sage

1 cup (4 ounces) shredded Chihuahua cheese*

If Chihuahua cheese is not available, substitute Monterey Jack cheese.

1 Preheat oven to 350°F. Spray 2-quart baking dish with nonstick cooking spray.

2 Cook macaroni according to package directions until al dente; drain and return to saucepan.

3 Meanwhile, melt ¼ cup butter in medium saucepan over medium-high heat. Whisk in flour until blended; cook 1 minute without browning, whisking constantly. Gradually whisk in milk in thin steady stream. Add ¾ teaspoon salt, nutmeg and red pepper; cook 2 to 3 minutes or until thickened, stirring frequently. Gradually add Cheddar and Monterey Jack, stirring after each addition until smooth. Add pumpkin; cook 1 minute or until heated through, stirring constantly. Pour sauce over pasta; stir to coat.

4 Melt remaining ¼ cup butter in small skillet over medium-low heat; cook until golden brown. Remove from heat; stir in panko, hazelnuts, if desired, sage and remaining ¼ teaspoon salt.

5 Spread half of pasta mixture in prepared baking dish; sprinkle with ½ cup Chihuahua cheese. Top with remaining pasta; sprinkle with remaining Chihuahua cheese. Top with panko mixture.

6 Bake 25 to 30 minutes or until pasta is heated through and topping is golden brown.

CHILI WAGON WHEEL CASSEROLE

MAKES 6 SERVINGS

8 ounces uncooked
   wagon wheel
   or other pasta

1 teaspoon olive oil

1 pound ground turkey
   or ground beef

¾ cup chopped onion

¾ cup chopped green
   bell pepper

1 can (about 14 ounces)
   stewed tomatoes

1 can (8 ounces)
   tomato sauce

½ teaspoon black
   pepper

¼ teaspoon ground
   allspice

½ cup (2 ounces)
   shredded Cheddar
   cheese

1 Preheat oven to 350°F.

2 Cook pasta according to package directions until almost tender; drain well.

3 Heat oil in large nonstick skillet over medium-high heat. Add turkey; cook and stir 5 minutes or until no longer pink. Add onion and bell pepper; cook and stir 3 minutes or until tender. (Drain mixture if using ground beef.)

4 Add tomatoes, tomato sauce, black pepper and allspice; cook and stir 2 minutes. Stir in pasta until coated. Transfer to 2½-quart casserole; sprinkle with cheese.

5 Bake 20 to 25 minutes or until heated through.

BAKED GNOCCHI

MAKES 4 TO 6 SERVINGS

1 package (about 17 ounces) gnocchi

⅓ cup olive oil

3 cloves garlic, minced

1 package (10 ounces) fresh spinach

1 can (about 14 ounces) diced tomatoes

1 teaspoon Italian seasoning

Salt and black pepper

½ cup grated Parmesan cheese

½ cup (2 ounces) shredded mozzarella cheese

1 Preheat oven to 350°F. Spray 2½-quart baking dish with nonstick cooking spray.

2 Cook gnocchi according to package directions; drain well.

3 Meanwhile, heat oil in large skillet over medium heat. Add garlic; cook and stir 30 seconds. Stir in spinach; cover and cook 2 minutes or until spinach is wilted. Add tomatoes, Italian seasoning, salt and pepper; cook 5 minutes, stirring occasionally. Gently stir in gnocchi. Transfer to prepared baking dish; sprinkle with cheeses.

4 Bake 20 to 30 minutes or until casserole is bubbly and cheeses are melted.

THREE-CHEESE PENNE

MAKES 6 SERVINGS

2 cups (about 6½ ounces) uncooked penne pasta

1 tablespoon olive oil

2 slices whole wheat bread, cut into cubes

2 cups (16 ounces) cottage cheese

2 cups (8 ounces) shredded Cheddar cheese

1 cup chopped plum tomatoes, divided

⅓ cup sliced green onions

¼ cup grated Parmesan cheese

¼ cup milk

1 Preheat oven to 350°F. Spray 2-quart casserole with nonstick cooking spray.

2 Cook pasta according to package directions; drain well.

3 Meanwhile, heat oil in large nonstick skillet over medium heat. Add bread cubes; cook and stir 5 minutes or until browned and crisp.

4 Combine pasta, cottage cheese, Cheddar, ¾ cup tomatoes, green onions, Parmesan and milk in medium bowl; mix well. Transfer to prepared casserole; top with remaining ¼ cup tomatoes and bread cubes.

5 Bake 20 minutes or until heated through.

PESTO LASAGNA

MAKES 8 SERVINGS

1 package (16 ounces) uncooked lasagna noodles

3 tablespoons olive oil

1½ cups chopped onions

3 cloves garlic, finely chopped

3 packages (10 ounces each) frozen chopped spinach, thawed and squeezed dry

Salt and black pepper

3 cups (24 ounces) ricotta cheese

1½ cups pesto sauce

¾ cup grated Parmesan cheese

½ cup pine nuts, toasted*

4 cups (16 ounces) shredded mozzarella cheese

Roasted red pepper strips (optional)

To toast pine nuts, spread in small skillet; cook and stir over medium heat 1 to 2 minutes or until lightly browned.

1 Preheat oven to 350°F. Spray 13×9-inch baking dish or lasagna pan with nonstick cooking spray.

2 Partially cook lasagna noodles according to package directions.

3 Heat oil in large skillet over medium-high heat. Add onions and garlic; cook and stir 3 minutes or until onions are translucent. Add spinach; cook and stir 5 minutes. Season with salt and black pepper. Transfer to large bowl.

4 Stir in ricotta, pesto, Parmesan and pine nuts; mix well.

5 Layer 5 lasagna noodles, slightly overlapping, in prepared baking dish. Top with one third of ricotta mixture and one third of mozzarella. Repeat layers twice.

6 Bake about 35 minutes or until hot and bubbly. Garnish with roasted pepper strips.

RIGATONI À LA VODKA

MAKES 4 SERVINGS

1 pound ground beef

1 jar (26 ounces) pasta sauce

1½ cups 3-cheese pasta sauce

4 cups (16 ounces) shredded mozzarella and Cheddar cheese blend, divided

¼ cup plus 2 tablespoons vodka

12 ounces rigatoni pasta, cooked and drained

1 Preheat oven to 350°F. Spray 3-quart casserole with nonstick cooking spray.

2 Brown beef in large skillet over medium-high heat 6 to 8 minutes, stirring to break up meat. Drain fat. Add pasta sauces, 2 cups cheese and vodka; cook and stir until heated through.

3 Place pasta in prepared casserole. Pour sauce over pasta; stir gently to coat. Sprinkle with remaining 2 cups cheese.

4 Bake 15 minutes or until cheese is melted.